first words

first words

Collected and Edited by Paul Mandelbaum

Algonquin Books of Chapel Hill

2000

Published by
Algonquin Books of Chapel Hill
Post Office Box 2225
Chapel Hill, North Carolina 27515-2225

a division of
Workman Publishing Company, Inc.
708 Broadway
New York, New York 10003

Library of Congress Cataloging-in-Publication Data
First words / collected and edited by Paul Mandelbaum. — Rev. ed.
    p.   cm.
Includes bibliographical references (p.).
ISBN 1-56512-272-0
    1. American literature — 20th century.   2. Youths' writings,
American.   I. Title: 1st words.   II. Mandelbaum, Paul, 1959–
PS508.Y68F57 2000
813'.540809283 — dc21   99-086208

2 4 6 8 10 9 7 5 3 1

For Hank and Rachelle

TABLE OF CONTENTS

Introduction ix

Margaret Atwood 3
Roy Blount, Jr. 17
Paul Bowles 27
Pat Conroy 43
Michael Crichton 47
Rita Dove 67
Clyde Edgerton 75
Gail Godwin 83
Allan Gurganus 99
Charles Johnson 109
Stephen King 117
Maxine Hong Kingston 123
Ursula K. Le Guin 133
Madeleine L'Engle 137
Jill McCorkle 145
Norman Mailer 153
Joyce Carol Oates 159
William Styron 175
Amy Tan 183
John Updike 187
Gore Vidal 215
Tobias Wolff 227

Appendix 231

WHAT WE HAVE HERE, AND WHAT WE DON'T

WHEN HE WAS FOURTEEN, John Updike, having long steeped himself in mystery novels, decided it was time to try his hand at one. He feverishly wrote forty-five pages and in the process created Manuel Citarro, the "dashing Spanish sleuth," and his secretary, Thomas Mays, an impetuous and delightfully naive narrator.

As a high school student, Joyce Carol Oates wrote a short story about a young boy longing to go fishing with his older brother, due back from the war. No serene union emerges, however, in this tale brimming with complex family secrets.

Norman Mailer, at the age of ten, was cranking out his action-packed adventure fantasy, "The Martian Invasion," in which the hero, Bob Porter, saws through the chains that imprison him, bops Martians on the head, and gleefully practices his French.

Not only did young Updike, Oates, and Mailer write those precocious pieces, but more important, such samples of their juvenilia still exist. Juvenilia, it turns out, have the regrettable tendency to become lost.

Many authors we wrote to in our research for this book replied to say their childhood efforts were no longer available, including Rita Mae Brown, Frank Conroy, Mavis Gallant, John Hawkes, Oscar Hijuelos, Harper Lee,

James Alan McPherson, Ann Petry, Scott Spencer, and Robert Stone. Julia Alvarez's were misplaced in some move, as were Sue Miller's. Tama Janowitz cited flooding in her mother's basement. A similar fate destroyed Lee Smith's first novel. Written when she was about nine, the work "featured my then-favorite people as main characters—Adlai Stevenson and Jane Russell. The *plot* was that they went West together in a covered wagon, then (inexplicably) became Mormons."

Laurie Colwin responded before her very premature death: "My juvenilia has been relegated to what Isaac B. Singer calls 'the vessel of mercy,' known to you and me as the waste paper basket." And Wallace Stegner reported before his death at age eighty-four: "Everything I have on hand was written after I was ninety."

Hortense Calisher no longer had the fairy tales she wrote at age seven. Nor could Tom Robbins put his hands on the *Snow White and the Seven Dwarfs* scrapbook filled with stories that he wrote when he was five and six. The magazines that Lorrie Moore and her brother used to assemble out of notebook paper and ribbon were also irretrievable.

Amy Hempel couldn't locate her bound grade-school volume *Mary Climbs the Mountain*. Likewise, Elizabeth Tallent had no luck turning up *The Postage-Stamp Horse*, her first book, "a novel set entirely on geranium leaves. The characters spring from leaf to leaf. Crayola illustrations. 3rd grade."

Joy Williams's mother had been doing some pruning in the family archives, and the author was "forced to admit" that the "small shrine" of juvenilia she had believed still in existence was no longer. Grace Paley tried in vain to find the ballad she wrote on the kidnapping of the Lindbergh baby, a subject "which struck me to the heart when I was about nine."

"I wish I had the play I wrote in the fifth grade, set in the first World War, that we put on in the classroom," replied Elmore Leonard, "but I don't."

And, prior to his death, James Michener sent his regrets as well: "Alas, I have no samples of my own early writing, and that's a shame, because when I was eight or nine I had my first encounter with Homer's *Iliad*, and when, in the final pages of the child's account of those heroic days, I learned that my Trojans had been defeated by a dirty trick perpetrated by the wily Greeks, I became so angry that I sat down, took a blue-covered examination book, and rewrote the ending of the Trojan War. I can assure you that though those pages are lost, in *my* version Ajax, Achilles and their bully-boys received what for!"

A few authors, though able to locate some juvenilia, were unwilling to see them in print. William Kennedy could not be persuaded to share his story "Eggs," which he had spoken about so temptingly at a PEN/Faulkner gala. Cynthia Ozick's juvenilia are sealed in a box in her attic labeled DO NOT OPEN UPON PAIN OF DEATH. And William F. Buckley, Jr., exercising similar caution, replied, "If I poked back at the stuff I wrote before age twenty-one I would almost certainly be driven to suicide, and I don't think the country could stand that premature loss."

Other potential contributions had been censored by outside parties. Mary Hood's grade-school novel about the westward pioneers was destroyed by one of her teachers, who "took one look and cried out, like a hay fever sufferer offered a bouquet of ragweed, 'Ridiculous!' and tossed the whole thing in the trash. I slunk away. I knew what she meant: 'Kid stuff!'"

But, as Mary Hood's teacher was not prescient enough to consider, the kid stuff of writers who grow up to achieve eminence can be another matter entirely.

J ANE AUSTEN WROTE FAR better as a teenager than most people ever
manage as adults. And she undoubtedly knew it. In August of 1792, in-
scribing her latest fictional creation to Cassandra, her adored sister,
the sixteen-year-old author wrote playfully:

> Madam, Encouraged by your warm patronage of "The Beautiful
> Cassandra" and "The History of England," which, through your
> generous support, have obtained a place in every library in the
> kingdom, and run through threescore editions, I take the liberty
> of begging the same exertions in favour of the following novel,
> which, I humbly flatter myself, possesses merit beyond any al-
> ready published, or any that will ever in future appear, except
> such as may proceed from the pen of your most grateful humble
> servant, the Author.

Contrary to Austen's jest, many others have written novels of greater
merit than the one in question, *Catharine*. Still, Penguin Classics saw fit in
1986 to include it with much of the rest of Austen's 90,000 words of existing
juvenilia—and a large portion of Charlotte Brontë's as well—in its august
series, alongside Homer's *Iliad* and Boccaccio's *Decameron*.

This act of canonization helped promote not only juvenilia's enter-
tainment value but also its literary significance. Childhood writing often
indicates an author's bent, demonstrating that each great novel is a chapter in a lifelong body of work. At surprisingly early ages, authors can establish a creative agenda: a theme, or a plot, or a voice—sometimes subtle,
sometimes not, but likely all the same to assert itself over and over again.
Retracing an author's steps back into childhood illuminates the creative
process behind the adult work.

In the Penguin Classics edition of Austen and Brontë, for example, editor Frances Beer notes the emergence of Austen's trademark moral criticism as it mingles with the youngster's earlier taste for pure ridicule—a taste that (fortunately) she never outgrew. Other scholars have also found Austen's juvenilia useful in charting her development. *Persuasion*, notes Donald Stone, has been commonly thought to "mark a new romantic element in Austen; and yet we see in 'Catharine' that it was there from the very beginning."

Like Austen, F. Scott Fitzgerald left some traceable literary fingerprints in adolescence. For example, two short pieces from his prep school days, "A Luckless Santa Claus" and "The Trail of the Duke," both feature hapless men playing the fool for frivolous women. In light of Fitzgerald's juvenilia, Daisy's appearance in *The Great Gatsby* seems in part destined, her creation the collaboration between an author at the height of his powers and a teenage boy groping to understand his own particular romantic bondage. Fitzgerald scholar John Kuehl, who points to several *femmes fatales* in Fitzgerald's life, remarks that "from childhood through marriage this kind of female fascinated him." Already she can be heard in the whimsical fiancée of "A Luckless Santa Claus," who makes such declarations as: "'Harry Talbot [. . .] if you aren't the most ridiculous boy I ever met, I'll eat that terrible box of candy you brought me last week!'"

Gustave Flaubert, whose extensive apprentice writings are preserved in three volumes, was also moved by teenage longing as he wrote juvenilia that would form a basis for his most famous adult masterpiece. At fifteen he completed "Passion and Virtue," which, says Lewis Piaget Shanks, is actually a "sketch of *Madame Bovary*." Its protagonist Mazza, dissatisfied with her drab husband, takes a lover in whom she invests great stores of passion ("she had an unquenchable thirst for infinite love," writes the young Flaubert). But after things go from bad to worse, she, like Emma Bovary, poisons herself, having similarly proved to be hopelessly maladapted to her world. Shanks connects Mazza's and Mme. Bovary's burning adulterous passions to Flaubert's teenage crush on a married woman, an episode that the writer refers to more directly in another work, written at about age sixteen, under the histrionic title "Diary of a Madman."

Flaubert already was experimenting with style at a young age, in particular the use of roving and ambiguous point of view, a technique for which he would later be studied. He is also famous for the gravity with which he devoted himself to his art, so it is not surprising, though a little alarming, to see this lifetime obsession already documented at age twelve in a letter to a friend: "If I didn't have in my head and at my penpoint a French queen of the fifteenth century, I should be completely disgusted with life, and long since a bullet would have set me free of this clownish pleasantry which is called life."

Childhood, especially for those of artistic temper, has not become fundamentally easier in the modern age. Paul Bowles, for example, perhaps in response to his early feelings of alienation, wrote voluminous juvenilia, and from these one can fashion a striking portrait of the artist as a wonderfully weird boy. He was partial to diaries (not of his own life, but of fictional characters), jotted down in a frantic headline style. The diary he wrote at age nine for the adventuresome Bluey Laber Dozlen begins: "Minnesota was erected. Bluey plans to come. Dolok Parosol stops her saying 'Marry me don't go.' Bluey gets mad. Dolok Parosol tells her again to marry him. She knocks him down. Bluey gets her things packed and puts on a beautiful blue sash. Bluey sails for Wen Kroy and lands. Bluey loves it."

And this all in the first five days! The next four months' entries outline many elements in Bowles's well-known novel *The Sheltering Sky* and his other adult writing. The impetuous, whirlwind travel is already present, as are punishing illness, romantic estrangement (the fact that Bluey can take a driving lesson on the same day her suitor "Dolok almost dies" seems to prefigure Kit's ability to betray her dying husband), and extreme climates (a 201-foot snowfall in "Bluey," the relentless desert in the adult work). As amusing as "Bluey" is, there is something unsettling about the pace of its plot, as though off the page lurks some void just waiting for the characters' first sign of inactivity—an undercurrent appropriate for a writer who would someday be called "existentialist to his fingertips."

Much as Bowles's existentialism was formed in childhood, so was Gail Godwin's fascination with religion. Her convent-school education, which seems so central to her 1987 novel, *A Southern Family*, also inspired a story written when she was fourteen. Though Godwin says she always enjoyed the school, and even fantasized about becoming a nun, the young protagonist in "The Accomplice" is terrified of strict Mother Blanche. "Nancy had feared Mother Blanche ever since that awful fall day when Mother and Daddy had deposited her at St. Catherine's," the story begins. In *A Southern Family*, convent-school nuns exert lingering influence on the lives of the other characters. And one nun in particular, Mother von Blücher, "famous for her ill temper," could be descended from Mother Blanche. "'Boy, she really hates us!' the little girls would exclaim, fascinated by her perpetual wrath"—so remembers Julia, who as an adult is now better able to understand the nun's complexity. Perhaps the ending of *A Southern Family*, with its prayer for Maria von Blücher, is a quiet, even subconscious nod from the adult author toward her teenage story.

Some patterns are downright haunting in their insistence. In Godwin's teenage story, Nancy dreams that she has pulled Jesus, suddenly alive, from a crucifix to help act out her revenge on mean Mother Blanche; about four decades later Godwin would write a scene in *Father Melancholy's Daughter* (1991) in which Margaret is awakened from a dream, only to be told that someone has sawed down the crucifix outside her father's rectory during the night.

Other patterns stand out for their contrast or irony. At about age twelve, Virginia Woolf wrote "Miss Smith," a sketch "making fun of feminism," according to Neville Braybrooke. "Miss Smith" is about a precocious girl, enamored of her own specialness, who grows up into an advocate of "Women's Rights." She finds herself lonely and unloved, however, until she renounces her former self and meets a gallant gentleman: "so much did she feel the need of someone stronger and wiser than herself that she consented to become his wife. So the two married like ordinary human beings [. . .]." Presumably still under the yoke of her Victorian upbringing, Woolf wrote this sketch apparently in utter earnestness, a striking antithesis to her later work. (She was constant in other ways, however: she chose the title "To the Light-House" for a sketch written at about age ten.)

Considering the acute individualism of Sylvia Plath's poetry, one imagines the contortions she must have suffered to write the formulaic story that *Seventeen* magazine published in 1950. "A date!" Plath writes in "And Summer Will Not Come Again." "Celia gulped, 'I'd love to!'" And yet the seventeen-year-old who could abide those words was also confiding in her diary that year: "spare me from the relentless cage of routine and rote. I want to be free [. . .]. I want, I think, to be omniscient. . . . I think I would like to call myself 'The girl who wanted to be God.'"

Before making his fame and fortune writing best-selling techno-thrillers such as *Jurassic Park*, Michael Crichton, while still a teenager, was cutting his literary teeth on *minimalism*, of all things. ("The day had left me depressed, and annoyed with people in general," concludes one story, "though I couldn't say exactly why. And that, in itself, was annoying.")

As for William Styron, whose novels are admired in part for the depth of their somber vision, we are pleasantly surprised to find him, at age seventeen, gamboling through a set of literary parodies in a pointed and mischievous satire of his school administration. "It is a College President, / And much surprised are we; / 'By that tailored suit and Arrow tie, / What shalt thou say to me?'" he writes, with apologies to Coleridge (whose brooding "Rime of the Ancient Mariner" was similarly preceded by such teenage amusements as "Monody on a Tea-Kettle" and "The Nose").

Juvenilia come in many forms. In her diaries, Anaïs Nin left a continuously traceable path of her personality and authorship all the way back to age eleven ("I notice no child in my class of my age thinks as I do," she reports in one undated entry from around age twelve). More recently, in the

1950s, fourteen-year-old Maxine Hong (later Maxine Hong Kingston) was using her journal as a way to flex her developing social criticism ("People just leave their manners at home when they come to dances it seems. [. . .] Priscilla heard someone make remarks about my pigtails [. . .]). Scraps of a diary Nathaniel Hawthorne is said to have kept in his teens are rich with compassion: He discusses a lamb he bought to save from slaughter, a bedraggled dray horse he conversed with, and a neighboring orphan, Betty Tarbox ("I love the elf because of her loss").

Depending on the writer and the nature of the correspondence, letters can provide tantalizing glimpses of an emerging writer. One registers the apparent relish with which seventeen-year-old Edgar Allan Poe relates the grisly details of campus life in a letter to his foster father. In describing someone's arm, wounded in a fight Poe had witnessed, he writes: "It was bitten from the shoulder to the elbow—and it is likely that pieces of flesh as large as my hand will be obliged to be cut out." And Chekhov as a teenager was already demonstrating a mellow wisdom beyond his years in a letter to his younger brother in which he urges: "you must be conscious of your dignity."

Journalism has been and remains one of the natural steppingstones for aspiring authors. W. E. B. Du Bois was writing for the *New York Globe* at age fifteen. Ben Franklin, at age sixteen, was sneaking letters to the editor into his brother's newspaper, under the pen name Silence Dogood. Between the ages of sixteen and seventeen, Samuel Clemens (later known as Mark Twain) contributed to his brother's newspapers about forty pieces. Many of them were attempts at the popular humor that characterized much of the newspaper contents of the day, and thus, writes Edgar Marquess Branch in *The Literary Apprenticeship of Mark Twain,* "Journalism determined his purpose, materials, and methods." In the Hannibal *Journal,* under the bombastic pen name W. Epaminondas Adrastus Blab, the sixteen-year-old Clemens took an opportunity to poke fun at the state legislature and to indulge in some plain old goofiness. As the sketch goes, in response to Blab's request to grant him a legal name change, "the Legislature was convened;

my title was altered, shortened, and greatly beautified—and all at a cost of *only a few thousands of dollars to the State!*"

More than a hundred years later, in a Georgia high school newspaper, sixteen-year-old budding humorist Roy Blount, Jr., would uphold the fine tradition of comic faux-reportage. In his column *Dear Diary by Joe Crutch*, he covers, for example, the public affairs of his student government: "(somebody had stepped on President Bobby DeFoor's nose, rendering him unfit for service)." From an earlier *Joe Crutch* report, we learn that, in the world of sports, "Zack Hayes got his head tangled in the net of the basketball goal." Oddly enough, three years later, comic-novelist-to-be Clyde Edgerton would, at the same age as Blount, make that very joke, in almost the exact same way, in his high school magazine in North Carolina.

Once in a very great while, child writers might even create work of unqualified literary merit. Edgar Allan Poe may have written his famous poem "To Helen" ("the glory that was Greece / And the grandeur that was Rome") as early as age fourteen. And Alexander Pope is believed to have first drafted his "Ode on Solitude" when only twelve years old. Walter de la Mare suggests in his 1935 study of childhood and juvenilia, *Early One Morning in the Spring*, that sometimes writers will return to material that in many ways they had dealt with more ably as teenagers. Authors—poets, actually—have even gone back and debased with their clumsy adult hands perfectly fine pieces written in youth, de la Mare goes so far as to say, citing regrettable revisions by Percy Bysshe Shelley and Abraham Cowley.

Not all readers are as charmed as de la Mare by the opportunity to compare an author's late work to an early work. "One of the worst habits of our day," one Austen scholar was arguing in 1931, "is that of fishing out of drawers and cupboards the crudities and juvenilities of authors who have subsequently written famous books."

Admittedly, there are some bad reasons to like juvenilia. For example, it would be a mistake to ascribe to childhood pieces more brilliance than they might actually possess, lapsing into the sort of hyperromantic atti-tude cautioned against by Myra Cohn Livingston in *The Child as Poet: Myth or Reality?* On the other hand, cruelty, or the desire to mock success-ful authors (as one contributor to *First Words* initially feared the anthology was set up to do), isn't a very productive purpose either. There is a much more reasonable motive—in addition, of course, to our quest for items of literary significance or our enjoyment at discovering the familiar in an unfa-miliar guise—and that motive is neither cruel nor coddling. It is our desire to connect with the person inside the artist.

To read the mystery novel—precocious and awkward at once—that John Updike wrote in early adolescence is to empathize with that young author's barely restrained excitement over his new role as creator.

Perhaps this sort of appreciation verges on being sentimental. Certainly to read young Robert Louis Stevenson imploring his father to let him come home from boarding school ("My dear papa, you told me to tell you when-ever I was miserable") strikes a slightly maudlin chord, as does a letter from the twelve-year-old Charles Dodgson (later Lewis Carroll) confessing that he can't find his toothbrush and so hasn't used one in "3 or 4 days" and end-ing with this plea: "Excuse bad writing."

We do excuse the bad writing. We are happy to. Anyone who has ever tried to plot out a short story of even modest originality can understand, for example, the forced results of Hemingway's revenge-in-the-wilderness tale "Judgment of Manitou," published in his high school literary magazine when he was sixteen ("Two ravens left off picking at the shapeless some-thing that had once been Dick Haywood [. . .]").

In this mood of fond affinity we pleasantly drift in and out of the knowl-edge that these young writers are the same people who have come to occu-py the places of greatest honor on our bookshelves. Juvenilia remind us of often forgotten truths: that art takes its nourishment from the common gar-den of human experience. And that authors are children grown up, still learning, even as they teach us.

Margin notes. In the margins of the text, readers will find side notes that make connections between the juvenilia and an author's life or adult work. When such a link pertains to a specific spot in the juvenilia, it is indicated by a pointer in the margin.

Ellipses. Virtually all the ellipses that appear in the side notes are the editor's, indicating where quoted material has been omitted. In very rare cases, ellipses are actually a part of the quoted material. In the juvenilia themselves, ellipses are always the author's unless they appear in brackets intended to give a clear indication that the juvenilia have been abridged or altered.

Mistakes. Editing the juvenilia, we have tried to adhere whenever possible to a sensible policy prompted by John Updike: we have silently corrected mere slips of the pen or of the typewriter keys, but mistakes that seem to reveal something about the development of the writer have been left intact. Even genuine mistakes, however, if they confuse the reader, have been corrected; in such rare cases, these changes are indicated inside brackets. When it seemed unclear what to do with an error, the author was consulted, though owing to the many intervening years since the juvenilia were written, this method was hardly foolproof. So despite the best of intentions and much painstaking effort, this process has sometimes been more intuitive than scientific.

Approximately half of the juvenilia in this anthology first appeared in some sort of school journal (most commonly a high school literary magazine). In the absence of manuscripts, we have applied the same principles of correction to the schools' typeset versions.

Dates. In cases where the juvenilia first appeared in school or other publications, a notation is made in the appendix, and the year listed with the text of the juvenilia refers to this original publication—unless the author recalled that the piece was written in a previous year.

The years included alongside references to an author's mature short stories are dates of first publication (except in such rare cases as we are aware of dates of composition), whereas the appendix provides the publication date of the collection the stories later appeared in.

ACKNOWLEDGMENTS

'D LIKE TO EXPRESS my deep appreciation not only to the authors who contributed juvenilia to this project but also to the following people for their guidance and aid: Alice E. Adams, Larry Baker, Geoffrey Becker, Jackson Bryer, Michael Cheney, Frank Conroy, Nicole Daya, Cheryl Friedman, Bernice Hausman, Mark Holt, Paul Ingram, Clair James, Betsy Keller, Brooks Landon, Tom Lutz, Richard Macksey, Fred Moten, Carol Offen, Kathy Pories, Kevin Potter, Margaret Richardson, Helen Ryan, Nancy Schwalb, Alan Sea, and Sharon Wood. And an extra thanks to Shannon Ravenel, whose encouragement and help have made working on this project a special pleasure.

—Paul Mandelbaum

first words

Margaret Atwood as a 14-year-old, pictured here at Niagara Falls

margaret atwood

W HEN MARGARET ATWOOD WAS in high school, she wrote about political repression, class inequality, and the difficult choices facing women—themes that continue to appear in her more than twenty-five published books of fiction and poetry. The author of *Bluebeard's Egg and Other Stories* (1983), *Power Politics: Poems* (1996), *Cat's Eye* (1989), and *Alias Grace* (1996), Atwood is perhaps best known for her 1985 novel *The Handmaid's Tale*, a futuristic nightmare in which an oppressive society classifies certain women as reproductive chattel.

Born in Ottawa, Ontario, in 1939, Atwood didn't write much as a child until age sixteen, "when it came to me that I was a writer." In much of the juvenilia below, she focuses on the very adult subject of regret: In "A Cliché for January," a young woman mourns a childhood friend trapped, by pregnancy, in an unwanted marriage. "The English Lesson," written when Atwood was seventeen, features a morose schoolteacher reflecting on the fiancé she lost to war and on the literary career that eluded her.

In a lighter mood, "Three Cheers for Corona" is a tongue-in-cheek essay (written as an English assignment) defending a woman's right to smoke cigars. As does so much of Atwood's adult work, this spoof takes aim at restrictive gender roles and strikes a blow for equality and flamboyance. ✑

A REPRESENTATIVE
(CIRCA 1956, AGE 15–17)

Atwood returns to ☞
the gutter in her story
"The Man from Mars"
(1977) when she refers
to an old man "who
lived for three years
in a manhole."

Sad intelligence, that seeks
Down dark and lone deserted streets
And through the sewerage of men
For one small spark, one ray of light;
He, the machine, enclosed in night
Potential, silent, still and sad
Lacks the power to use the power
To drive the wheels to make him mad.
Inertia, curse of everything
That wants to grow, to reach and stretch,
Has laid its thin sciatic hand
Upon this sorely crippled land.

THREE CHEERS
FOR CORONA!

"I did smoke cigars a
couple of times, on a
'dare,'" says Atwood.
"They made me ill."

(CIRCA 1956, AGE 16–17)

For some time now, my name has been drifting
through a sooty cloud of misunderstanding and prej-
udice. My erstwhile friends avoid me on the street, I
hear strangers whispering about me as I pass, and my
acquaintances regard me with raised eyebrows and a
supercilious curl of the lip.

Why? The answer is reasonable enough. I smoke
cigars. Mind you, I don't publicize the fact. When
offered a cigarette, I lower my eyes modestly and
murmur a polite, "No, thank you." Then I brace
myself for the inevitable question: "Don't you
smoke?" My upbringing compels me to tell the truth.
"Well, not exactly. At least, not cigarettes. Only
cigars." This usually brings an amused but obviously
disbelieving smile; but the smiles vanish when I slip

my stoogie out of my purse, lick it all over to counter-act dryness, chomp off the end with my little yellow incisors, and light up. Astonishment is hardly the word for the reaction.

There are many arguments against women smoking cigars. I have heard them all, and have concluded that they are, without exception, weak, inconclusive, and based on the shaky foundation of conformity. Most people contend that smoking cigars is unfeminine; it is hardly worth the space to point out that short skirts, short hair, and short marriages, all established facets of present society, were once frowned upon. Another popular fallacy is the one that confines the use of cigars to middle-aged, paunchy business executives. There is no reason why women, who are now participating actively in the business world, should not inherit the cigar along with the seat on the Control Board. As for the pale, quavering neurotic boys (I refuse to call them "men") who, while fumbling in their pockets for matches, and opening their cigarette cases with shaky, nicotine-stained fingers, *dare* to tell me that cigars are bad for the health — they are merely pitiable. Anyone who maintains that one medium-sized cigar every two weeks is more harmful than a pack of cigarettes a day is flying in the face of logical reasoning, mathematics, and known facts, and is not even worth arguing with. My little weakness is held to be "something that just isn't done," and therefore undesirable. But it *is* done: I do it.

The advantages of being a cigar-smoker far outweigh the disadvantages. Cigars have all the good qualities, and only a few of the bad ones, of cigarettes. For instance, cigarettes give you "something to do with your hands." So do cigars; but, whereas cigarettes only occupy *one* hand, it takes two, and some-

Even in this high school essay, Atwood displays a keen awareness of the sexual-political freight attached to everyday items and gestures. In her dystopian novel The Handmaid's Tale, *Atwood's enslaved protagonist describes, with an anthropologist's curiosity, the high-heeled shoes worn by tourists as "delicate instruments of torture. The women teeter on their spiked feet as if on stilts, but off balance; their backs arch at the waist, thrusting the buttocks out."*

In Atwood's novel The Edible Woman *(1969), we're introduced to Duncan: a pale, 26-year-old (he looks 15), "compulsive neurotic," cigarette-smoking "boy," who delivers such garden-variety pronouncements as, "The only thing about laundromats . . . is that you're always finding other people's pubic hairs in the washers."*

times even three hands to keep a good cigar under control. Cigars are soothing and relaxing; (the beginner should take care *not* to relax on the floor). No one could stand too many cigars in succession; therefore, the danger of becoming a slave to the habit is slight. And they certainly separate the sheep from the goats as far as friends are concerned: only the most faithful and loyal of friends will venture to be seen in public with a cigar-smoking female. (I admit it was rather a shock to discover that I hadn't a true friend in the world; however I'm glad to be rid of them — the hypocrites!)

But the best reason — the reason without which all the others would be as useless as a well at the bottom of a lake — the culminating triumph of a reason, resulting from years of torturing self-analysis and mental research — is a simple one.

I enjoy them!!

Care to join me?

This sort of breezy commentary on social convention developed into one of the more provocative tones of Atwood's adult voice.

1 9 5 6 — A N D   F O R   E V E R
(CIRCA 1956, AGE 16–17)

There is no room for giants on this earth
The petty people swagger, strut, and preen,
Gathering gold with avaricious claws.
All thoughts except the trivial wilt and die;
True joy has gone, there is but shallow mirth;
The rich are worthless, and sharp envy green
Moves them to cram still more their full-filled paws;
The poor are only born to toil and cry.

In The Handmaid's Tale, *society's most oppressed are forced to work at toxic-waste dumps, "the way they used to use up old women, in Russia, sweeping dirt."* ☞

THE ENGLISH LESSON

(1957, AGE 17)

Miss Murdock adjusted her thick, steel-rimmed glasses in front of the mirror. She regarded the reflection before her: her own familiar shapeless face with its wispy frame of brownish-gray hair (those wisps would never stay in place—she had ceased to try); the green leather armchair in the corner; the legs of Miss Spencer, the History teacher, who was dozing by the window with her shoes off; and the mirror on the opposite wall that reflected her own reflection. If there were three mirrors, she thought, I would see a whole line of Miss Murdocks, one after the other, all moving together like puppets. She wondered idly why Miss Spencer, who was fifty-six if a day, wore red nail-polish on her toes. She dabbed powder on her biscuity cheeks with her fluttery, irresolute hands, applied her lipstick (unevenly, as usual), in a thick, dark line and blotted most of it off, twitched her pearls and flicked a few crinkly hairs from her collar. I really don't know why I bother, she thought; struggle, struggle for survival like an amoeba in a glass dish, without purpose, without direction. Miss Spencer stirred in her sleep as the door wheezed shut.

Outside the Lady Teachers' Room, Miss Murdock plodded down the hall with her habitual wavering gait. There was a time, far back, when she had marched erect—shoulders back, chin up, toes pointing straight ahead—but it was too much effort now. The bell went, and students spurted into the hall. Where was she going? Where? Oh yes—Room 6, 10B English—her worst class. Without anticipation, without enthusiasm, without fear, practically without thinking, she would teach grammar rules for half an hour to 10B; then lunch, then classes, then another night and another day. I am a dried-up well, she thought, with dry dead moss around the edges.

She reached her classroom. Everything was as usual. The swell of noisy talking, the muffled cries of "Here comes the sheep!!" suddenly stilling as she entered, her own feeble, vacant smile, her bleated half-plea, half-command to open books, all the same, day after day, for ever and ever, world without end. Mechanically, she began to take up the homework, even though she knew four-fifths of the class had not done it.

"John and I (was, were) going to the store."

Where was John now? Is there a heaven? She heard her own words, made familiar by memory, coming from afar: "Not yet, John; I want a career first; I want to finish college, and go to Europe for a year; maybe work on a newspaper. But perhaps in a few years. . . ." And then the war and good-bye. And then the letters—ten, fifteen, twenty of them, a line of letters—a line that ceased abruptly, to be followed, it seemed a minute later, by one more—one more letter, edged in black. She had cried then. She never cried now.

A boy in the back row slipped a note across the aisle. A girl tried not to giggle. Miss Murdock ignored them. She realized that her pupils did not respect her for her laxness, her mental laxness that sagged like the ring of fat about her waist and the flabby, freckle-covered muscles at the backs of her arms. She tried to tell herself that it was not good to force children to pay attention, that their interest would develop spontaneously in time, but she felt uneasily that this attitude was just a not-too-effective excuse for her laziness.

"I (will, shall) write a letter to-night."

Even though Atwood grew up during the 1950s, "when marriage was seen as the only desirable goal" for a woman, her parents did not pressure her to marry, she once told Joyce Carol Oates in a New York Times *interview.* ☞

To write. To write had been to live. To write she had saved and scrimped, scrimped and saved, rejected the bright, gay clothes she had once been so fond of, put herself through college, hating her poverty, waiting for the day she would be famous. . . . She could not pinpoint the exact moment when her resolution had deserted her. It had flowed from her in days of drudgery at the office of the newspaper that had hired her, in nights of remembering, in rejection slips from weekly magazines. Finally she had clutched the once despised security around her and fled to the sheltering shadow of the local high school. . . . . fled from the limelight of life to the semi-shade of a slow death. This fertile cultivated ground was to her a flat, sterile plain, devoid of life, productive only of a monthly pay-cheque. The meaning of her life had seeped through the sand, and she was left wandering in a desert between the dawn that would never come and the sun that had already set.

Miss Murdock sighed. Her class was doing its utmost to be annoying, she reflected. She smiled her feeble smile and continued with the lesson.

"He (ate, eat) his lunch, (which, who) was very good."

Lunch. In five minutes—no, four—the bell would ring for noon-hour dismissal. In her mind's eye, she saw herself descending the stairs to the cafeteria, in the faded print dress that looked like a housecoat and didn't fit; she saw herself buying her sandwich and coffee and sitting down opposite Miss Spencer in the Teachers' Dining Room; she heard Miss Spencer chirp something about the weather, and saw herself smiling her weak smile—smiling vacantly as she watched the coffee dribble down the side of the cup, smiling and smiling through the days of darkening shade, for ever.

Rennie in Bodily Harm *once wanted to be a serious reporter but finds herself writing more and more fluff. She describes a desertion of will that caused her to see her "ambitions . . . as illusions."*

Literary critic Clifton Fadiman remarks that in Atwood's story "The Man from Mars," the author "never raises her voice, yet the desired effect of mingled pathos and irony registers perfectly." Passages from "The English Lesson" have not yet achieved this level of understatement, but "A Cliché for January" (see page 10) seems an early experiment in such restraint.

A CLICHÉ FOR JANUARY
(1959, AGE 19)

Atwood takes special pleasure in satirizing the banality of commerce. In The Edible Woman, *Marian works for a market research firm and must survey consumer response to such advertising phrases as "deep-down manly flavor."*

☞

Damn, she thought, as she climbed the last step. Mrs. Carter.

She dropped her bus ticket into her purse and fumbled for it, to give herself time to think. I could pretend not to see her—no—too late for that—or get off at the next stop—she weighed fifteen minutes in the rain against Mrs. Carter, and Mrs. Carter won. Bus too empty—can't sit somewhere else. She's beaming at me—she knows I see her. Well, here's for it. Colours flying high for the good of the cause.

Mrs. Carter's smile broadened as she approached. Your smile always reminds me vaguely of a halitosis ad, she thought, or one of those little back-pages-of-the-newspaper ones about false teeth. She gave herself an internal twist, and felt the pattern click into place.

— "Oh, hello, Mrs. Carter, how are you?"

— "Well, Diane, how are you?"

— "Just fine, thank you," as she sat down.

Slight pause. The acrid smell of damp wool rose from her coat in the warmth of the bus. Think, you fool. The inevitable topic.

— Its real nasty weather to-day, said Mrs. Carter. You must have got real wet. On days when its storming like this I always say how lucky I am cause we're right outside a stop and I can wait till I see it coming, you know, and just run out and get it. But you have to wait, don't you. It must be just terrible on days like this."

— Oh, it isn't too bad. I don't like the drizzle, but I like sliding on the ice if I'm alone and have boots on.

She felt Mrs. Carter twitch at the word "sliding", and draw back slightly. Watch it, she thought. Keep to the surface, damn it.

—How is your dear mother? I see her at most of the Home and School meetings, you know, when I go that is. Your little brother's in Grade nine now isn't he? How they grow up! My Robert, he's in Grade 12 now and I can hardly believe it.

Why don't you call him Boop? All his friends do—I mean its *done*. But of course, *Robert* is so much more distinguished.

Mrs. Carter was staring vaguely at a large pink placard advertising girdles. She said, in a somewhat softer voice:

—"Seems like just yesterday you and Myrna was in Grade 12 together."

Myrna.

What did you do with yourself, Myrna? You were really quite clever in Grade 12. You used to do things, too; I remember those drawings you always made in your margins. They were good. The teachers didn't like it, though.

Her feet were getting uncomfortably warm inside her flight boots. I hate the smell of damp feet in flight

Margaret Atwood at age 20, reading poetry at the Bohemian Embassy in Toronto

A Cliché for January

Oh~~, oh~~ Damn, she thought, ~~when she~~ as she climbed the last step. Mrs. Carter.

She dropped her bus ticket into her purse and fumbled ~~around~~ for it, to give herself time to ~~think~~. I could pretend not to see her — no — too late for that — I ~~could get~~ got on get off at the next stop — she weighed fifteen minutes in the rain against Mrs. Carter, and Mrs. Carter won. Bus too empty — can't sit somewhere else. She's beaming at me — she knows I see her. Well, here's for it. Colours flying high for the good of the cause. ~~She dropped her ticket~~ as she approached.

Mrs. Carter's smile broadened. ~~I~~ ~~see~~ Your smile always reminds me vaguely of a halitosis ad, she thought, or one of those little back pages - of - the - newspaper ones about false teeth. She gave herself an internal finish, and ~~she~~ felt the pattern click into place.

—"Oh, hello, Mrs. Carter, how are you"?
—"Well, Diane, ~~just~~ how are you?"
—"Just fine, thank you; as she sat down.
Slight pause. The ~~dry~~ acrid smell of ~~damp~~ wool rose from her coat in the warmth of the bus. Think, you fool. The inevitable topic.
—Its real nasty weather today, said Mrs. Carter. You must have ~~gotten~~ real wet. On days when its storming like this I always

5.

Soft, passive...

the seat). My God ...

My God, she thought ...
Mrs. Carter, Mrs. Carter ...
... your silly-created pattern ... She got up ...

Mrs. Carter opened her eyes
weakly. She made an effort:

— It's been so nice talking to you,
Diane. say hello to your mother
for me, won't you?"

Outside it was still raining, in a
heavy, misty. the snow was
melting ... rapidly. She stood with
her feet in the slush, and
listened to the gush of the sewer
beside her.

the water said pity pity pity
pretty pity as it trickled down
the drain?

— end —

Peggy Atwood
Jan. 23, 1959

boots, especially on buses, she thought. She took off her gloves.

Silence. Two minutes of silence while we take off our gloves and remember the dead.

I wish we could take off our boots too, and slide on the watery ice with our bare feet. But that wouldn't be nice. She thought of Mrs. Carter on the ice with no boots and pink feet like the girdle ad and smiled with the far corner of her mouth.

The half-anxious, half brittle voice which rippled the image was hardly Mrs. Carter's. It sounded as if it were being strained through a seive.

—You know that Myrna's—married—now?

Yes, I know that Myrna's married.

—Yes! Last month, wasn't it? It must have been a lot of excitement!

"This is the pregnancy tip-off," explains the author. ☞

Mrs. Carter relaxed. Thinks I don't know. Yes, I know.

—She worked for a while, you know, but I guess every girl wants to get married sooner or later, and she really wasn't all that keen on her job. . . . Dave is really such a nice boy. . . she trailed off.

That "nice" is in red neon capitals, of course. No, it would be better in italics, or small black type in a letter to the manufacturer of a patent cough medicine beginning "I shall always be grateful for the relief. . . ."

A new gush. "We're really *so* happy. . . . it was a lovely wedding", in a minor key. Then, with a pathetic attempt at condescension:

"You're still going to school, aren't you?"

—Yes, College.

—Well, that's very nice . . . though I don't know— for a woman—'course men can always use an education for their life work, you know, but you can't learn to cook no matter how many books you read." She squeezed out a parody of her usual laugh.

"Yes, I suppose that's so." Keep up the front; good girl.

There was a longer interval; the bus lurched through a puddle.

Suddenly she was aware that Mrs. Carter was crying. Her eyes were closed and she was sucking her lip, her hands loose, her whole body slack against the seat.

My God, she thought, and felt an outward surge . . . Mrs. Carter Mrs. Carter, there's nothing I can . . . your self-created pattern . . . you wanted . . . She got up. [. . . ?]

Mrs. Carter opened her eyes weakly. She made an effort:

—Its been so nice talking to you, Diane. Say hello to your mother for me, won't you?"

*   *   *   *

Outside it was still raining, in heavy misty drops. The snow was melting rapidly. She stood with her feet in the cool slush-filled gutter and listened to the gush of the sewer beside her.

The water said pity pity pretty pretty pity as it trickled down the drain.

Margaret Atwood

"The pregnancy is why Mrs. C. is crying," explains ☜ the author.

☜ This paragraph in the manuscript is so heavily revised that even the author finds it impossible to decipher completely.

Atwood shows continual curiosity about words, their sounds and the way they tumble over one another ☜ to make meaning. "Waste not want not," Offred writes in The Handmaid's Tale, *and then proceeds to examine the maxim afresh: "I am not being wasted. Why do I want?" In* Bodily Harm, *Rennie recalls that at age 8 she thought a "molester was someone who caught moles."*

Roy Blount, Jr., at about age 16

roy blount, jr.

GROWING UP IN DECATUR, Georgia, Roy Blount, Jr., fantasized about a place where "movies and the federal government and magazines came from and where they argued about books." As early as high school, he had clear sight of his vocation as a literary humorist, but after graduating from college in 1963 he discovered that he'd overestimated the need for his services. "This was partly because I was not as good at Humor as I had been in high school and partly because of the historical moment."

Eventually, however, he would rise to become one of the country's foremost wags. The author of more than a half-dozen published books of fiction, essays, and memoir, including *What Men Don't Tell Women* (1984), *First Hubby* (1990), and *Be Sweet: A Conditional Love Story* (1998), Blount's work has also appeared in scores of magazines. His career, in one critical appraisal, has been compared to Mark Twain's.

Blount's writing style is highly personal, tangential, allusive, and on easy speaking terms with literary tradition (one Blount essay makes the case for Walt Whitman as a locker-room sports reporter). Although he was born in Indianapolis, in 1941, he spent most of his childhood in Decatur and plays up the southern elements of his voice, which is at times homey, genteel, or mockingly crude. Appropriately, in view of our interests here, his writing has been called "at once adult and adolescent." It is also often extremely funny, as the following remarks explaining his disappointment in his own juvenilia confirm:

> Maybe my mother saved the wrong things. I know she threw away all my *Mad* magazines because she found them too erotic. Or maybe I should blame my children: they got into my box of juvenilia, picked out all the magical passages, copied them in their own hands and burned the originals. At any rate, I am too principled to pass their surviving early work off as my own.

> So I represent myself with highlights of my earliest journalism, largely fictional. I was sixteen and seventeen, writing two columns ("Roy's Noise" and "Dear Diary by Joe Crutch") and various other things for the Decatur High School *Scribbler*. You would be in a better position to appreciate these items if you had known Mrs. Ormston and Kenny McNeely, as my readers then did. Mrs. Ormston was the physics teacher, determined to catch up with Sputnik. Kenny McNeely looked like Opie only round.

> Here also, from my senior year (Class of '59), is the first thing of mine to appear in a national publication (*The Beta Club Journal*). This apologia for not playing varsity football strikes me as overly self-deprecatory, in retrospect, and I fear that it may provoke glib theories as to why my first book, written fifteen years later, was about hanging out with the Pittsburgh Steelers. Yet I submit it, selflessly.

> (Ah. It just now hits me that I am older than the writer of that book by more years than he was older than the *Scribbler* writer. Never mind. I'll be all right.)

> I might mention that if you are a juvenile writer, and on reading these selections you feel you have not yet attained this level of sophistication, and therefore you despair of ever developing into an author of sufficient stature to be included in an anthology of juvenilia, you should bear in mind that these are the *best* things I could find. The worst, and even the next worst, are less promising than anything you or anyone else has ever written. Nothing could persuade me to share with you any of my extremely long 1958 Christmas poem, for instance, beyond this representative couplet:

As a Frenchman would say, *"bon* grief" —
We've nearly forgotten to herald Greg Moncrief.

I must have thought that anything was possible.

If on the other hand you are a youngster who feels that you
personally would never consent to the publication of anything as
immature as these writings even now, much less once you have
reached the height of your powers, my response is this:

Yeah, sure. You wish. ✑

SCIENCE FAIR IS MISERABLE FLOP
(1958, AGE 16)

The annual Science Fair was held on March 5th, 6th, and 7th, and was acclaimed by one and all as a miserable failure. All of the projects turned out to be either fakes or not good enough, and no one had a good time. In fact, during the scuffle following the disqualification of Elaine Porter's project, an ultrasonic high frequency fordomatic grunch, for the fourth straight year (this disqualification and ultimate brawl has become an annual occasion and cupcakes and punch are usually served afterward); Mrs. Hammet received a nasty gash on her forehead and four biology students and an as yet unidentified bystander were trampled to death. Also, one of the judges was blown up when someone crammed a cherry bomb into his ear after he went to sleep.

Among projects that figured in the judging for awards was an invisible small-mouth bass which Ronnie Shutley had bred by crossing a grizzly bear and the common garden pea. (Crossing a grizzly bear is not advisable for the amateur.) Of course the judges had to take Ronnie's word for the fact that the fish was there.

"I can't believe that this was my semi-colon," says the author. "But I suppose some desperate measure ✑ seemed called for."

In First Hubby, *Blount focuses his wit on some proposed arts projects: Verna Passevant's "The ✑ Songs of Mosquitoes and Flies," T. P. Fullilove's "Criticizing Clouds," and Foley Bigelow's "Carrots in the Shapes of States: An Attempt to Grow These Root Vegetables So as to*

Resemble Vermont, New
Hampshire, Illinois,
Idaho, Virginia, Kentucky
and Tennessee on
Purpose."

Joan Givens was about to be awarded the grand prize for her excellent study of Neanderthal Man when the bulk of her project turned out to be Gordon Cranford watching a butterfly.

Jean Fell had what looked like an excellent project coming along. She put two mice in a cage and fed one of them sauerkraut, orange Kool-Aid, and creole limas.

First prize was awarded to a new student, Nikolai Kopek. Nikolai constructed a very nice earth satellite. (We regret to state, however, that Nikolai was not present when the decisions of the judges were announced. It seems the F.B.I. wanted to ask him a few questions.)

The exclamation point,
says Blount, "doesn't sound
like me either." ☞

Edwin Jelks was awarded second prize for his superb scale model of Mrs. Ormston, and he made a very nice acceptance speech! He said that he was "honored" and that he wished to thank "my fellow students, Mrs. Ormston, and the entire faculty; all of whom helped me tremendously with my project, and most of all, my father, who made it."

ROY'S NOISE
(1958, AGE 16)

Watching early football practice, I came upon a surprise in the form of a first-string guard. Don't know whether or not it was because a yellow shirt couldn't be found to fit him, but Bobby Anderson was playing with the first team. No, not against them. With them. We of The Scribbler think Bobby is a living memorial to what perseverance, hard work, and lack of competition can do for a man.

There is one phase of the football half-time ceremonies that has caused me no end of wonderment (actually, I haven't lost any sleep over it, but I have to fill this space some way), and that is the fact that the majorettes are *always* smiling. I have watched the faces of generations of twirlers (another lie—I seldom look any higher than their legs), but I have yet to see one frown. I have seen them drop their batons six or seven times hand-running, swallow flies, knock the stuffings out of their corsages with their batons, almost lose their little skirts, and be bitten by dogs, but never yet has one frowned just a little. They may be grinding their teeth and swearing inside, but they never show it on the outside. I may be in the minority, but I believe I would feel immensely better if I saw just one little scowl on the face of a majorette while she was going through her routines during the half-time.

from

DEAR DIARY BY JOE CRUTCH

(DECEMBER 1957–FEBRUARY 1959, AGE 16–17)

Nothing particularly interesting happened today in school. Jack Crider accidentally hoisted himself up the flagpole while trying to raise the flag. Zack Hayes got his head tangled in the net of the basketball goal. Just those little everyday things that go into a regular school day.

Dick Gear's absence from school for the past two weeks hadn't aroused much comment up to now, but it has taken on a new light now since it was found that the Student Council funds have been reduced to a 1902 Indian Head Penny, a badly tarnished medallion bearing the head of Francis Tarkenton and a six-year subscription to the American Poultry Journal.

Before becoming a professional quarterback, Francis Tarkenton was a star athlete at nearby Athens High School, which competed against Decatur. He was two years ahead of Blount.

I am forever being amazed by the grace and agility of Kenny McNeely. The other day, for instance, while marching smartly toward the rifle range (in better step than anybody), he slipped on some ice, slid a good fifteen feet, and ended up flat on his back underneath a parked car. The last time I passed by the scene he was still there, still at a perfect port arms.

U.S. Vice President Clementine Fox becomes "Leader of the Free World," in First Hubby, *after a thirteen-pound fish mysteriously drops from the sky, killing President DaSilva.* ☞

Speaking of the Junior-Senior, the Junior girls voted, en masse, at a recent class meeting, not to invite dates from other classes. The boys, who would have outvoted the girls, had it not been for the fact that Nancy Butcher, class V.P. (somebody had stepped on President Bobby DeFoor's nose, rendering him unfit for service) counted the votes, and that Tommy Lucas and fourteen other boys were asleep and didn't vote, claim the girls are afraid of competition.

Mrs. Ormston's class fired off a rocket today. Unfortunately, it missed Mrs. Ormston, and the whole class had to stay in after school and write, "I will not shoot no rockets at Mrs. Ormston no more." 500 times. When Mrs. Dieckman heard about it, she made Mrs. Ormston write, "I will not use incorrect grammar no more." 500 times. What would Werner Von Braun think?

Wernher von Braun (1912–1977), rocket scientist. ☞

"HUH-uh Mffff Mfffff." "FWOO." "Ooo-laaaaaaah." And so ☞ *the lovers in* First Hubby *achieve sexual union, as Blount displays his ear for phonetic humor.*

I had an exam this morning. A French exam, no less. I'm pretty good at French (hinky dinky parlez vous; ou, la, la; B.B.'s pour moi), but my grades don't reflect the fact. But I know one French student who passed with flying colors though he knew only one French phrase—"Mademoiselle McGeachy, vous etes losing weight, n'est-ce pas?"

YOU OUGHT TO
BE IN FOOTBALL

or "Young Man, Why Aren't You in the Service?"

(CIRCA 1958, AGE 16)

Probably the most prevalent delusion existing among adults today is the deep-seated conviction that any high school boy who has more than one leg and is worth his salt plays high school football. Late last summer this fact was brought out clearly as I cut the grass of a neighbor. For some reason, he was trying desperately to make idle conversation over the frenzied roar of my lawnmower. (The word "roar" does not cover at all adequately the sounds made by my lawnmower. My lawnmower makes various sounds, all very loud and unpleasant. Come to think of it, the lawnmower itself is very unpleasant, and I kick it frequently. But I digress—and about time, you will say, if you are still listening.) Suddenly the neighbor had an idea: "Ah!" he said to himself, "this big strapping youth must certainly play football. I will talk to him about that."

So, willy-nilly, he began to talk about it: "Well, Jimmy, (this, as you no doubt have noticed, is not, and was not, my name; but I have, and had, forgotten his name, too, so I don't, and didn't, mind) how is football coming on?" he said confidently, his face lighting up. I looked at him somewhat blankly and ran over a gladiola. "Football," he reiterated, after an awkward pause. "You do play football, don't you?" "No," I said, simply. After waiting tensely for a few seconds for me to explain that football was against my religion, or that I had a wooden foot or something, he asked, incredulously and with a touch of horror creeping into his voice, "Why?" He had me there, so I just mumbled a little and ran over another gladiola. After staring in utter, open-mouthed disbelief, and with a "should this boy be cutting my grass?" look in his eyes, the neighbor went back into his house. He left my pay on the front step, I haven't been invited back, and he now herds his children in the house whenever I pass by.

Pro football dressing rooms "had always made me nervous," Blount confesses in About Three Bricks Shy of a Load *(1974), his behind-the-scenes account of a season spent with the Pittsburgh Steelers. "I had never liked being around a lot of people each of whom could so easily beat me half to death that there wouldn't be any point to it."*

Surprisingly enough, the fact that I don't play football has never kept me up nights worrying, and I don't cower with shame when a gridiron hero passes by in the halls at school. By the same ticket, then, I have also never figured out why I don't play football; I just don't. After my aforementioned little interview, however, I have given it a little thought.

When I say I don't play football, I don't, of course, mean that I have never played football. I just don't play organized football. And I have played some of the organized brand. In the seventh grade, for instance, I was a scrappy 93-pound guard (I am tempted to say that a 93-pound guard has to be scrappy, but actually I wasn't particularly scrappy—I just threw that in because it reads good) on the grammar school team. I also went out for football in eighth grade. I did some calisthenics, ran a little, watched some of the others scrimmage, and didn't come back the second day. Since then my participation in high-school football has been strictly vicarious.

*This bronzed look doesn't come easily, as Blount explains in ☞ * Not Exactly What I Had in Mind. *"I go to a nearby tannery every spring, lay out twenty-eight dollars and a little something for the attendant, and have myself dipped."*

Actually, I tell myself, I am not exactly the football type. I have always considered myself more the lean, bronzed, woodsman type. However, since I used to get homesick on Boy Scout camping trips, I peel easily, and I am finding it increasingly necessary to pull in my stomach, this illusion does not hold up too well. Probably my best excuse for not being a gridder (not that I need one, mind you) is the fact that I am too light for the line and too slow for the backfield.

Also, I'm chicken.

ROBOT GOES BERSERK

87 Perish as Monster Roams Streets

(1 9 5 9 ,   A G E   1 7)

In a flurry of excitement last week, the Science Club robot broke from his moorings in T.M. Johnson's basement and escaped to peril the entire population for forty-eight hours before he was captured.

Franticly flinging its arms, singing "Charlie Brown," singeing everything within reach with its flame thrower, the monster wreaked havoc on the city streets, killing eight-seven men, women and children, injuring 114 others, and causing an estimated $47,000 worth of damage.

Unfortunately, the first call for the police came while the entire force was engrossed in a pinochle game, and no one answered the phone, but within twelve hours the men in blue were out hunting the monster, and finally they cornered him and finally destroyed him. The monster left in his wake scores of corpses and tremendous destruction. An added tragedy was revealed when Mrs. Ormston announced that everyone who worked on the robot for his science project would get an "Incomplete" on his permanent record.

In First Hubby, Dr. Dingler, the founder of Dingler College, also invokes the classic threat against youthful transgression: "Things can be made to show on people's pummanent ☞ reckuds."

Roy Blount, Jr.

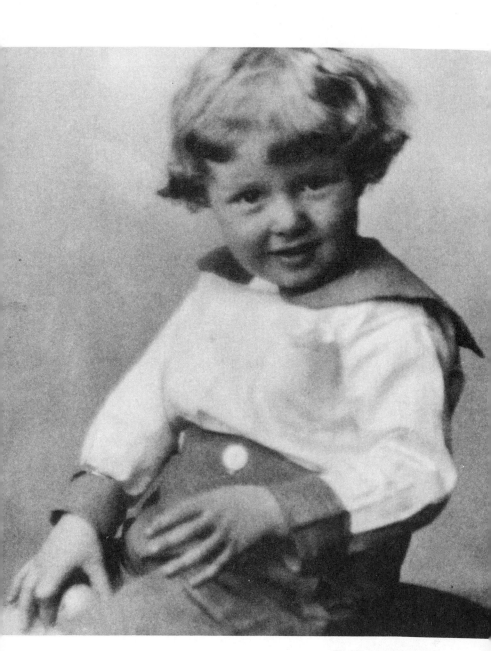

Paul Bowles at age 2 or 3

paul bowles

T HE LATE EXPATRIATE AUTHOR and composer Paul Bowles is
known for haunting tales set around the world, particularly in
North Africa—his home for most of his life. The author of more
than a dozen published books of fiction, including the novels *Let It Come
Down* (1952) and *Points in Time* (1982) and numerous short-story collections, he is perhaps best known for his first novel, *The Sheltering Sky* (1949),
the story of an American couple whose marriage decays far away from the
security of home. Alienated from others, from themselves, and from their
surroundings, many of his characters lead dreamlike—or nightmarish—
lives, thus inviting a comparison to Poe, whose stories transfixed Bowles as
a child whenever his mother read them to him.

Born in 1910 in Jamaica, New York, Bowles was five years old before he
had any significant contact with other children. Of all the eccentric, critical, sickly, or unpredictable adult relatives that people his autobiography
Without Stopping (1972), Bowles's father stands out as a problematic character. The dentist's animosity toward his newborn son supposedly ran so
deep that the man once set the infant Bowles in front of an open window
during a blizzard (or so, Bowles recounts, his maternal grandmother once
told him). Years later, at the age of nineteen, Bowles returned the favor, to
his own surprise, by throwing a meat knife in his father's direction.

The young Bowles retreated into his own imaginative world whenever
possible. One of the by-products of this was reams of juvenilia: stories about
animals, written when he was four, maps of an imaginary planet (around

age seven), diaries about imaginary characters (see below), a daily newspaper featuring dispatches by foreign correspondents, a pseudo-opera (see below), and melodramatic stories his seventh-grade classmates would stay after school to hear him read.

At one point his grandmother exhorted Bowles to rid himself of some of his copious creations. "No, no! I have to have them all," he said. Despite such youthful resolve, sadly only a little remains today. ✑

A LETTER
(1915, AGE 4)

Seventy-three years later, spiders are still objects of his scrutiny. "I have a spider whose behavior mystifies me," Bowles notes in his journal. ☞ In the intervening years, he named his 1955 novel The Spider's House (a title taken from the Koran).

Dear Miss Anna.

Thank you for the erector. I have been making letters with it. Monday the 3rd I was playing with a little yellow spider, but he was so tiny that I lost it.

Do you notice my Red Cross sticker, and my other little Santa Claus?

Love from Paul.

THE LADY OF PEACE
(1917, AGE 6)

Bowles employs another malicious, talking animal in his darkly humorous fable "The Hyena" (1960), in which the misfit protagonist outwits and kills the conventionally proper stork.

One day when the Lady of Peace was out walking, she met a cat.

"My word! What a pretty cat," she said.

The cat looked at her kind of queer, then said: "Go home."

"The idea! I won't," said the Lady of Peace.

"Hike it home," said the cat.

"I won't!" cried the Lady of Peace, stamping her foot.

"If you don't go home, I'll make you," said the cat, throwing some stones.

"After all, I don't think it's such a pretty cat," said the Lady of Peace, and went home.

POOR AUNT EMMA

(CIRCA 1919, AGE 8)

Poor Aunt Emma, sick in bed
With an ice-cap on her head.
Poor Aunt Emma, sick in bed!
She's very sick, but she's not dead.

Bowles describes the manuscript of "Poor Aunt Emma": "It's made into a little booklet, about 1½ inches by 1½ inches, with only a few words in block letters on each page. On the last page it says: «The End. If you want more, apply to Paul F. Bowles.»"

LYRICS FROM "LE CARRÉ," AN "OPERA"

(CIRCA 1919, AGE 8)

Oh, lala,
Oh daba,
Oh honeymoon!
Say, oh say when . . .
But she got no further
For there was her ex-husband
Glaring at her like a starving pussycat.

Love triangles complicate a number of Bowles's works, including his celebrated story "In the Red Room" (1981), which, according to John Updike, "presents, at a level of understatement almost beneath thermal detection, that original hotspot, the Oedipal triangle."

GIVE ME WINE

(C I R C A   1 9 1 9 ,   A G E   8)

*Bowles grew up during
Prohibition, a subject of
some debate between his
father and paternal grand-
father. As an occasional
motif in his adult work,
the consumption of alco-
hol takes on special
significance against the
backdrop of Muslim
cultures.*

Give me wine, give me wine
That comes from a vine
Hanging in a garden of thine.
Oh, no! You'd get drunk.
Yes, you would, you rank old skunk.
You'd yell and yell
Until the bell of jail would ring:
Bring him, bring him.
I'll give you some molasses
Served in little glasses,
But never any wine.

BLUEY

(1 9 1 9 – 2 0 ,   A G E   9)

*Bluey Laber Dozlen was
one of Bowles's favorite
imaginary diary subjects.
Bowles wrote these entries
in newspaper-headline
style because "that seemed
to me the most adult
way of presenting the
material," he recalls.*

1919 December 1919

26. Minnesota was erected. Bluey plans to
    come.
27. Dolok Parosol stops her saying "Marry me don't
    go." Bluey gets mad.
28. Dolok Parosol tells her again to marry him.
    She knocks him down.
29. Bluey gets her things packed and puts on a
    beautiful blue sash.
30. Bluey sails for Wen Kroy and lands.
    Bluey loves it.
31. Bluey thought this country was heaven.
    Bluey writes to Dolok.

*Wen Kroy: ☞
New York spelled
backward.*

1920 January 1920

1. Dolok sails for Wen Kroy and gets wrecked.
2. Dolok got back to Wen Kroy. Bluey welcomes him.
3. Bluey gets an awful cold, and gets into her bed.
4. Bluey feels a little better. Dolok comes to see her. Bluey cries.
5. Bluey was worse. Doctor says she has Pneumonia. She faints.
6. Bluey feels better and gets up. Dolok gets diptheria.
7. Dolok gets worse. Bluey gets a Pierce Arrow Automobile.
8. Dolok almost dies. Bluey weeps. Bluey takes a lesson in running her auto.
9. Bluey has a blowout. Dolok dies. Bluey faints.
10. Dolok had funeral. Bluey goes. Mrs. Jobestor dies. Red Cross Day.
11. Bluey shuts herself in the closet all day long. Dolok is buried.
12. Bluey buys a new tire. Bluey takes another lesson on her auto.
13. Bluey goes out to ride in the auto and gets frozen.
14. Auto runs on four hundred miles still frozen.
15. Auto runs fifty-eight miles and gasoline runs out.
16. 37 degrees. Bluey comes to. Faints when she finds herself.
17. Bluey comes to. 37 to 39 degrees. Bluey gets some gas.
18. 40 to 41 degrees. Bluey starts for home and goes one hundred miles.
19. 39 to 40 degrees. Bluey gets home again.
20. 30 to 31 degrees. Bluey gets a bad cold. Henry Altman visits.
21. Bluey falls in love with Henry. Bluey worse.

In The Sheltering Sky, *Port becomes seriously ill, and his skittish wife, trying to determine the malady, runs through her knowledge of diseases: "Diphtheria began with a sore throat, cholera with diarrhea, but typhus, typhoid, the plague, malaria, yellow fever, kala azar—as far as she knew they all began with fever and malaise of one sort or another. It was a toss-up."*

Bluey's frantic movements prefigure Bowles's own dizzying international itinerary recorded in Without Stopping.

22. Bluey worse. Doctor says she has pneumonia.
23. 21 degrees. Bluey better. Henry Altman calls again.
24. Bluey better. 20 degrees. About five o'clock it begins to snow.
25. Snow worse. 18 degrees. Bluey all right. Bluey goes to call on Henry.
26. 16 degrees. Great blizzard in Chicago. Bluey stays at Henry's.
27. 12 to 14 degrees. Great blizzard arrives. Bluey still at Henry's.
28. Bluey tells Henry she loves him. Henry tells her he loves her.
29. 10 degrees. Bluey gets snowed in has to stay at Henry's.
30. 6 degrees. Blizzard worse. Henry wants to marry Bluey.
31. 2 degrees. Bluey wants to marry Henry. Blizzard covers everything.

1920 February 1920

1. 0 degrees. Bluey and Henry get engaged. Blizzard worse.
2. Snow covers all the houses up. 1 degree below zero at noon.
3. It stops snowing. 0 degrees. Bluey still at Henry's.
4. 3 degrees. Snow starts to melt. Bluey wants to marry Henry.
5. 5 degrees. Snow still melting. Bluey tries to dig through.
6. 6 degrees. Bluey digs and digs. Snow stopped melting.
7. Bluey finds out she has dug a block under the snow.
8. Bluey and Henry dig some steps up and land a block away.

9. 13 degrees. Bluey uses that way to get home. Henry goes with her.
10. 15 degrees, Bluey feels bad. It snows. Bluey reads "Hovertis."
11. Doctor says Bluey must get weighed once a week. Bluey yells.
12. Bluey gets weighed 95 lbs. 19 degrees Bluey goes back to Henry Altman's.
13. They get snowed in again. 2 degrees. Bluey reads and gets a headache.
14. Bluey's headache worse. 23 degrees. Henry worries.
15. Bluey and Henry get out. 25 degrees. Bluey's headache all right when she gets out.
16. Bluey and Henry go ice skating. Henry falls down.
17. 29 degrees. Bluey goes home again. Henry goes with her.
18. 31 degrees. Bluey says she loves Henry. Henry almost faints.
19. Bluey weights 95½ lbs. 33 degrees. Bluey says she wants to weigh 186.
20. 35 degrees. Henry digs out the house. Bluey helps him.
21. It starts snowing again. 34 degrees. Bluey wants a child.
22. Henry says they cannot have a child until they get married. 31 degrees.
23. Bluey says in seven weeks she will marry Henry. Henry faints.
24. It still snows. 25 degrees. Bluey goes back to Henry's house.
25. It snows and hails 22 degrees. Bluey has a headache stays in bed.
26. 19 degrees. Bluey gets up. Henry tells her to marry him.
27. 16 degrees. Bluey has a fight with Henry. Bluey yells.

This excerpt from the Bluey diaries is reprinted as it appeared in a 1943 issue of View *magazine, to which the adult author was a regular contributor. "For pure comedy, dramatic tension, and harmonic development of theme," according to the magazine's contents page, "it seems unequalled by any other work by a writer of the same age, and needless to say, is far more persuasive than the writing of most adults."*

28. Greatest storm in world's history. 13 degrees.
Bluey knocks Henry down.
29. 10 degrees. Bluey hits Henry. Henry hits Bluey
and gives her a black eye.

1920 March 1920

1. 8 degrees. Bluey tries to get out but snow is 108
feet high.
2. 5 degrees. Bluey breaks down and cries and
forgives Henry.
3. 6 degrees. Henry forgives Bluey. Bluey still cries
and cries.
4. 8 degrees. Still snowing and hailing snows 86
feet that day.
5. 9 degrees. 195 feet of snow. Bluey weighs 96½
lbs. Henry is so mad he has a fit.
6. Bluey starts crying again. 10 degrees out. 197 ft.
of snow.
7. Still snowing and hailing. 8 degrees out. 198 feet
of snow.
8. Bluey reads "Da Lod help ma." Bluey laughs so
she has a pain.
9. Henry finds out there is no food in the house.
10. Bluey tries her best to shovel out but cannot.
11. Bluey faints of hunger. Henry eats a live cockroach.
12. Henry faints of starvation. 201 feet of snow.
13. The cat dies of starvation. 20 degrees out.
Still hailing.
14. Bluey and Henry both unconscious. 21 degrees
out.
15. It stops snowing. 200 feet of snow. Robbers try to
get in.
16. 194 feet of snow. Dolok Parosol's mother gets a
cold.
17. 192 feet. She is worse. 24 degrees. Robbers try
to get in.

18. 192 feet. Robbers get in and don't find anything. 23 degrees.
19. 190 ft. Dolok's mother is worse. 26 degrees.
20. 188 ft. Doctor says she has Pneumonia, she faints. 28 degrees.
21. 186 ft. She is worse. She tries to get another doctor.
22. 180 ft. She gets another doctor. 30 degrees at twelve o'clock.
23. 174 ft. The other doctor says she has the influenza.
24. Dolok Parasol's mother dies of grief for loss of Dolok.
25. 163 ft. Dolok Parasol's sister weeps and weeps for her mother.
26. 160 ft. Bessie still weeping.
27. 154 ft. Bessie gets influenza.
28. 147 ft. Mr. Parasol gets influenza. Bessie worse.
29. 137 ft. Mr. Parasol gets crazy. Bessie worse.
30. 127 ft. Mr. Parasol almost dies. Bessie has Chrisis.
31. 117 ft. Mr. Parasol wishes he would have chrisis. Bessie better.

1920 April 1920

1. 110 ft. Mr. Parasol has chrisis. Bessie better.
2. 101 ft. Mr. Parasol dies. Bessie allright.
3. 91 ft. Baker comes and stuffs a roll down both of their throats.
4. 72 ft. Bluey and Henry come to and thank each other.
5. 70 ft. Henry kisses Bluey, Bluey kisses Henry. He faints.
6. Bluey and Henry get out. Snow still 62 feet.
7. 60 ft. Bluey and Henry find 7 billion dollars, divide it.

In other entries, Bluey "becomes a spy. . . . learns how to play bridge and smoke opium . . . and is last seen hiding out in Hong Kong from a vengeful housemaid she was once foolish enough to dismiss," describes the author in Without Stopping.

"I regularly settled into protracted illnesses with a shiver of voluptuousness at the prospect of the stretches of privacy that lay ahead," Bowles writes of his childhood, in his autobiography.

8. 51 ft. Bluey gets $3,500,000, gets an aeroplane.
9. 45 ft. Henry gets a beautiful car, Packard.
10. 34 ft. Bluey says she will live and keep house for Henry.
11. 30 ft. Bluey gets a maid. Lina Minner. Bluey faints.
12. Bluey Dozlen & Henry Altman get married. 21 ft. Bluey faints.
13. They go on their honey-moon. 18 ft.
14. 57 degrees 6 ft. They go to Niagara Falls.
15. 2 ft. Bluey weighs 99. Bluey faints.
16. 1 ft. They go to Thousand Islands.
17. 6 inches. Bluey says she will stay at Thousand Islands.
18. 2 inches. Henry doesn't want to.
19. Snow melts entirely away.
20. Houses all flooded in Ridgefield.

The travel tugs of war between Bluey and her lovers seem to anticipate the author's own frequent negotiations with his wife, Jane, as recounted in Without Stopping. ☞

Paul Bowles, as a teenager in the late 1920s

ENTITY

(1927, AGE 16)

The intimacy of spirals has become stone to him. This is in reality only the last prayer urge. As it is, all the crimson of stamps has resolved into loops. These fold up and seek sounds beyond lime rinds.

Let is not be understood that the frenzied fingers were here wishing us to leave. It was only that he went away and shells returned. An urn of disgust cannot stop up the pores for they are after his creases of intelligence. Or, let us say, if one end were rubbed blue and all edges left green we should have a pleasing effect. But all this is uncertain. One does not feel the imperative qualities soon because behind lapels there are buttons of unrest.

Eradicate, if you can, the adaptability of my nature to joy. It is our heritage, this abandoned cerise;—perhaps the only one we have left. The steel of now cannot be rounded like letters of the system into laughing hordes of misunderstanding. We cannot permit these unflinching bones to perform such elegies. There may be abysms in our fingers. There may be falsehoods about ponds. Last leek occurred a strange step. Paradise stalked, and seizing a trombone from the wall, stumbled. In this way all such margins weaken.

Can you not all discover how ennui will creep thus? There is no object in such flight. Masses have power.

At any rate, I shall not have panted entirely beyond borders of limpness. Our sycamores need repose. Is it possible that ever we shall be able to trace our responsibilities to such commands? We cannot ignore successfully the call of feathers. We must heed somewhat bristles. As it is, we are not entirely beyond

Inspired by Breton and the surrealists, "Entity" was written during a period in which Bowles avoided "conscious intervention. . . . The material itself, being beyond my control, also escaped my judgment, but this did not matter; the important thing as far as I was concerned was that no one seeing it should guess that I was only sixteen," he recalls in Without Stopping. *The piece appeared (in 1928) in* transition, *a hot Paris literary magazine, which also published James Joyce and Gertrude Stein.*

aluminum fences. This is the reason for his dialogue. The origin of power is everywhere.

If any such enmity is discovered let us discard our yawning.

The susceptibility of emotionalism to unguarded caves may be readily realized by all of us. His smiles fall slowly into jars of porcelain. Even if his pain persists, all these losing forces discover their positions.

Much of Bowles's adult work is concerned with the tenuous nature of consciousness, reality, and meaning. In "A Distant Episode" (1945), a linguistics professor has his tongue cut off by nomads, who then imprison him as their jester, negating whatever meaning his life may have had.

A rubber is black. The eternal verities are not. In this effigy we may discern a long boulevard. Leaves of such tendencies shall impale him, and he will be certain to remain poised over lavender pebbles.

The immutability of spheres is constant. All about us are carcasses of planets. Whirling continues a short while. Close her eyes and fold her hands above. We are ready for the treatise on hexagonal tiles.

When all shall have been immersed in brass, it will be easily recognized. Only then shall the grain of the pelt be held by fundamental hands. The only tense is the future and futility is taken for granted.

A WHITE GOAT'S SHADOW

(1929, AGE 18)

"A White Goat's Shadow,"
which appeared in Argo,
a student magazine, is
the author's first published
piece of fiction. It was
adapted by Bowles from
a longer, stream-of-
consciousness account
of his trip to Paris.
Concerned chiefly with
"flow," the young author
was afraid that a more
careful approach to the
writing would shut him
down, he recalls in his
autobiography.

Dinner was to be at two thirty and I was invited to accompany the duc and his brother to a nearby café for an apéritif. It is not yet created for me the Paris café. We sit on the terrasse and I see sawdust on the floor. The sun is bright but there is a heaviness somewhere in me. A nostalgia already? What are you having? Quick, buck up. Show your teeth and smile saying same as you. Trois amourettes. You like Paris? Yes forcé I think I am going to like it. I know. I am going to love it. The bread is strange lying there in the basket. The three glasses arrive on white saucers pricemarked. My God, it's anisette. Ce n'est pas tout-à-fait la même chose. Oh, but I've passed out on anisette and after you've passed out on anisette you can never taste it again. But I gulped a third of it and felt it percolate upward into the convolutions. I haven't eaten since early this morning in Boulogne. I'm sorry. I can't drink any more. They are worried. Don't drink it they say. Don't drink it. The traffic is becoming a roar. The city is sweet-smelling. I relax and spread my legs under the little table. A long sigh goes out from my lips. You are tired? says the duc solicitously. Yes and awfully hungry. What? he asks. Very tired, very hungry I repeated with French accent. Yes yes he nods understanding. We are going to eat presently. The city is spread far out away from and around me. The sun seems near. It is slowing down. A painful ralentir like the Pacific 231 coming to a halt. In between the beats I feel an agony. It has always been like that. When I have been delirious it is the horror of the two conflicting tempi that makes my hands sweat. The taxis trumpet too gaily. I suddenly want to weep; to wake up. I close my eyes stoically. If I press the lids together too tightly two tears may roll out. I cough casually; blow my nose. Open. They have drained their pernods and are eating the bread. The duc offers me a cigarette. I take it pushing back my chair. The sudden motion makes me want to dance. I feel my ankle muscles contract involuntarily. We will return to my mother's says the duc rising. I walk elastically. The sun shines. I notice that the trees have little iron fences around them and that above the fences they are budding. They are farther on their way towards the spring here than in the country on the way from the boat. As we reenter the apartment I am already feeling at home. The dinner is heavy. Pitchers of wine red and white. America is dead. Long live the Etoile.

Sipping Pernod in a drab North African town, Port declares, in The Sheltering Sky, *that he'd "still a damned sight rather be here than back in the United States."* ☞

II

"The quotation marks and the parentheses at the margin were clearly a European affectation which I must have considered chic at the time," explains the author.

"A white goat's shadow. They were walking down the "shale steps during the next reincarnation and he "was ahead of them so that they dared to discuss him. "The lake was blue and the woods shrieked with "locusts. In the fields the dust quivered with heat and "all the grass was dead but on the east verandah it was "cool with the venetian blinds let down all around. "They were sitting in deck-chairs sipping bacardis. As "he entered they frowned slightly and continued to "sip. This will never do. Blast them. Take me back to "my other life."

It is difficult to live. Slowly the dusk fell to a serenade of taxi-horns. It is the supreme test to be alone the first evening surtout after an April when the twilight is scented with adolescence. Pang pang says the night as it falls quietly layer upon layer. I am so tired. The world is just coming out of ether. A passive spirit. Twenty francs a day is too much because at that rate I shall have that makes oh my God what shall I do? I do not eat, neither do I sleep. But later ca sera (mieux. At Boulogne after two in the morning down (stamped an Americaine shouting I must have a (bathroom adjoining my room. I'm sorry Madame (there are none. It's ridiculous. There must be some. (I've got to have one. Upstairs it is quiet. The curtains (at the window are heavy. The cord pulls them back (to show the basin outside. The empty place at night. (The strange little lights around the place. Two men (trot allegro laughing. They are lost. A fog is coming (in. A whistle out on the Channel. Frisson and sigh. (Pull back the cord and undress. It is too late to sing. (Go to sleep.)

👉 *Many uncomprehending, inflexible, or obnoxious travelers make their way across Bowles's fictional landscape. Tunner, who brings an especially inimical ugliness to* The Sheltering Sky, *announces, "'One thing I can't stand is filth.' 'Yes, you're a real American, I know,'" counters Kit.*

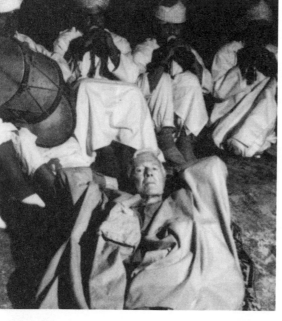

Paul Bowles

Pay Conroy, standing between numbers 22 and 24, on the Beaufort High 1961–62 basketball team. ("It's hard to tell that Southern schools were segregated back then, isn't it?") Randy Randel stands last on the right.

pat conroy

P AT C ONROY, WHO WAS born in 1945 in Atlanta, moved about once a year throughout his "ruined and magnificent childhood." After growing up under the thumb of his Marine Corps father, Conroy would later write out some of the emotional turmoil he'd been storing. Whether the subject is the appalling educational conditions on a South Carolina island where he once taught (recalled in his 1972 autobiographical account *The Water Is Wide*) or family tyrannies—explored in his novels *The Great Santini* (1976), *The Prince of Tides* (1986), and *Beach Music* (1995)—Conroy taps great reserves of passion.

The many readers of his books can recognize a recurring personality in Conroy's work: the playful smart aleck, the iconoclast struggling against malevolent authority, the "bona fide cracker boy" who has stretched beyond his limited horizons. Perhaps most central to that personality, and the aspect represented below, is the spirited poet yearning for expression.

In a recent letter, Conroy describes his poem "To Randy Randel," written while the author was a high school student in Beaufort, South Carolina. (The other poem included here—on the same subject—was the author's first attempt at verse.)

> I found this poem by accident in 1989 when I was visiting my high school English teacher, Eugene Norris. Gene is one of those life-changing figures in my life whom I still keep up with and try to thank at least once a year for the unimaginable generosity they showed me as a child. We were going through his collection of Beaufort High School yearbooks and came across the poem to Randy Randel.

Randy and I had sat beside each other in Mr. Norris's English class and had become good friends after playing football, basketball and baseball together and sharing a teenage joy in teasing Mr. Norris. Randy's father, Morgan, was the superintendent of schools and Randy used to tell Gene: "Treat me kindly, Norris. Give me high marks, or I'll have your job."

Randy was a splendid athlete who could throw a football seventy yards, had a beautiful touch on a jump shot, and who everyone thought would one day pitch in the Major Leagues.

Conroy goes on to describe the first baseball game of Beaufort High School's 1962 season, in which his friend, after striking out five of the first seven batters he faced, mysteriously collapsed and died "and changed the lives of all of us on that field forever.

"I like it very much that my first urging toward art came at a time when a friend died and my heart was broken and I wanted to drop a note to the world. This poem means a great deal to me and lets me know what kind of boy I must have been. I wish I'd been a better poet then. . . . no, I don't." &

Conroy presented this poem to the Randel family shortly after Randy's funeral. It now hangs in their house, and the Randels have kindly sent a copy of it for inclusion here.

In Memoriam
To a Dear And Cherished Friend

Tall and limber as a tree in the wind
Sinews growing, and muscles to tend
Why did the Lord so mighty and strong
Pick Randy out of this plentiful throng?
The Lord released a snow-white dove
Go, go get Randy, the Randy I love
Bring this child to my judgement-seat
I want to caress this young athlete
Tell his mother and father to wait
For they will meet again at the golden gate.

Pat Conroy
March 15, 1962

TO RANDY RANDEL

(1962, AGE 16)

I have ceased to wonder at the rapid flight of day.
The slice of birds and winters shout
Are but an effort meant to render nature praise.
Myself I wish to think about
A hundred friends who walk a pathless street alone
In search of lost and youth-grieved dreams.
Once a boy, fluid-limbed and not quite fully grown
Gave love to life and life it seems
Surfeited with the honey tooth of perfect joy
Yet darkness lit another place
Far off among the hills. So shadow wrapt the boy
In death and pressed his guiltless face
Into the flawless pages of eternal rhyme,
A snow fleeced lamb of earth and God bound child
    of Time.

In The Water Is Wide, *Conroy's account of his year spent teaching impoverished kids on a coastal island, he recalls Randy Randel's death. "I watched Mr. Randel as he looked into his son's face and felt his son's heart and held his son's hand," he writes. "And in that instant was born the terrible awareness that life eventually broke every man. . . ."*

The author notes the influence of Thomas Wolfe.

Pat Conroy

Michael Crichton at age 20 (in front of window), listening to Marianne Moore at Harvard

michael crichton

MICHAEL CRICHTON WAS AN early achiever. At sixteen he managed to publish in the *New York Times* a travel article about his family vacation. To help put himself through Harvard Medical School, he cranked out thrillers published under the pseudonym John Lange. He also wrote an award-winning mystery, *A Case of Need* (1968), under the name Jeffrey Hudson. (Part of Charles I's court, Hudson was a famous dwarf; the use of his name was in winking reference to Crichton's own towering height.) Still in medical school, Crichton became a best-selling author at age twenty-six with *The Andromeda Strain* (1969), published under his own name. He has increased his fame with eleven subsequent novels—including *The Terminal Man* (1972), *Jurassic Park* (1990), and *Airframe* (1996)—which excel at spinning technical research into gripping plots. In addition to directing a few movies (among them *Westworld*, 1973, and *Coma*, 1978), Crichton has also written several nonfiction works that demystify medicine and computers for the general reader. He also created the Emmy Award–winning TV drama, *ER*.

Although he completed medical school, Crichton decided not to go into practice, because, among other reasons, he says, his fantasy life was too strong. In his essay "Quitting Medicine" (*Travels*, 1988), Crichton explains that he used to listen to patients' stories for material for his fiction writing. "I was not behaving like a doctor that *I* would want to consult. So I thought I ought to quit."

Born in Chicago in 1942, Crichton says he wanted to be a writer from early childhood. His father, a journalist, was an influence, with his impressive bedtime stories and an ability to illustrate them on the spot. Crichton recalls, in *Travels,* a third-grade assignment to write a puppet show, for which he created a "nine-page epic. . . . My father said he'd never read anything so cliché-ridden in his life (which probably was true)," writes Crichton. "This hurt me and confirmed a pattern of conflict between us that persisted for many years."

The author himself is critical of these early samples of his work. "As you will see from the selection," he notes, "I have been unflinching." ☙

J O H N N Y   A T   8 : 3 0

(C I R C A   1 9 5 7 ,   A G E   1 4)

The bad guys had him, Johnny had to admit,
Trapped in a winecellar, black as a pit,
Outside were the villains, forty or more,
And the only thing keeping them out was that door.

The heroine, too, was trapped in the dim,
John had to protect her, no matter what happened to
        him,
Now they were breaking the door down and with
        a rattle,
John drew his sword, and prepared for the battle.

And now the door was splintered,
And the multitude poured through,
But John promptly skewered them,
And flicked them all askew.

The much relieved heroine let out a long sigh,
The villains were dead, and with a wave of goodbye,
John jumped on his horse and into the sunset so red—
Turned off the television set and went up to bed.

In The Terminal Man, *Crichton has Dr. Ross hear gunshots coming from Harry Benson's hospital room, shots that we soon learn are coming from the TV. This mild manipulation of reader expectations is a more subtle variation on the joke Crichton is playing with here.* ☞

UNTITLED

(1960, AGE 17)

*During his high school
years, Crichton wrote a
lot on the side. ". . . I
suppose it was really a
form of self-therapy. I had
tremendous energy; I was
getting something out,
though in retrospect I
can't clearly see what.
I do remember that I had
a great interest in trying
to be spare. Minimalism
rearing its youthful head."*

"Well?"

"Well what?"

"Well, what did you find out?"

"Nothing."

"Really?"

"Not a thing."

"No kidding. That's a tough break."

"Yeah."

"You mean, you went to talk to him, and he still
didn't say anything?"

"Yeah."

"Well, didn't you pry a little and try to find out
what's going on?"

"Of course. That was why I went."

"And he wouldn't talk."

"Not a single word. And I was over there for
nearly an hour. I couldn't stay any longer and have
him figure out what was coming off."

"Yeah, that's true. . . . Have you talked to the girl?"

"What girl?"

"Julie or whatever her name is."

"Oh—yeah, I did. Or, at last I tried to."

"She have anything to say?"

"Nothing much."

A silence.

"Looks like you got problems, kid."

"Hell! I just wish I knew."

"Nobody else talked to you about it at all?"

"Nope."

"In other words, you don't really know if it's true
or not."

"Yeah, I guess so."

"Maybe he doesn't know anything about it
either. Maybe that's why he didn't mention it. Was
he friendly?"

"Yeah, he was friendly. I mean, as friendly as he ever is. You know, like always."

"Did he give you any funny looks or stuff like that?"

"I don't know. He's always giving me funny looks. Ever since I've known him he's been giving me funny looks. He just kind of stops whatever he is doing and looks at me like he was trying to figure a math problem written on my forehead. You know that funny stare he has."

"No, I never met him."

"Oh. I thought you had someplace. Lots of guys know him—more than you think."

"Yeah, I know quite a few guys that met him, but I never have."

"Well, he has this real funny stare. And he's never completely serious anyhow. You can never tell whether he's serious or whether he's just kidding around."

"You scared?"

"I don't know. Would you be?"

"You mean if I were you?"

"Yeah."

"Probably."

"And what would you do, if you were me."

"Hell, I don't know. I don't have any idea. I mean, I never thought about it."

Crichton no longer remembers what this story is about. "For a long time, the most common criticism of my writing by teachers was that it was too unclear—or too subtle. (For better or worse, that is no longer a criticism that is made!)"

LIFE GOES TO A PARTY

(1961, AGE 18)

The party was noisy, red, loud and laughing, and despite himself, Mark enjoyed it. He stood leaning against a wall, off in one corner, and he watched. It was a typical Joan Gilbert party, with lots of room and lots of people and lots of little bits of food and cookies and rather heavily spiked punch. In a way, it was like all the Gilbert parties he had been to during high school, and in a way it was not. Now, everybody there was a freshman in college, back for their first Christmas, so it was a big sophisticated reunion, with all the guys smoking brand new pipes and all the girls trying hard to show that they had, in their own way, been equally enlightened.

Of course, nobody was paying any attention to the fact that five days earlier, Jerry Barnhill, who had been in their graduating class in high school, had been on the plane that had crashed over Brooklyn, splattering metal and skin all over the apartment houses. After all, he was buried now, so what the hell.

Not that he, Mark Heggerman, leaning against the wall with a glass of champagne punch which he had further fortified by a quiet trip to the Gilberts' bar, was thinking about Jerry Barnhill. Jerry Barnhill was not particularly any friend of his. Not at all.

From across the room he saw Joan Gilbert, weaving through the little knots of guests, stopping momentarily to talk and laugh with one or another of them. She was wearing a red dress, and she looked good in red, and she wasn't bad looking anyway. Mark smiled; it was good to see her again.

She returned the smile. "Well," she said. "I didn't see you come in. You must have been late. Are you going to stay late?"

In Rising Sun, *Peter Smith doggedly investigates the death of Cheryl Austin, who is described by the business leader hosting a huge party one floor below the murder scene as "a woman of no importance."*

Crichton's high school yearbook offers the following profile: "Big Mike," "journalist," "Honor Society," "Latin Scholar," "basketball star," "that different laugh!" and "a verbose intellectual"

Mark bowed. "Your wish," he said gravely, but it didn't turn out so well because he spilled part of his drink when he bowed. The liquid hit the wood floor noisily.

"Say," Joan said, laughing. "How many have you had?"

Mark felt confused. "I'm sorry," he said. "Where can I get a cloth to clean it up?"

"You can't. It doesn't make any difference anyway. Just put that drink down and dance with me."

He did, and was surprised that they could slip so easily back into the old groove again together. She curled her hand up behind his neck the way she always did, and dropped her head on his shoulder, and it was all just as if they had never stopped.

"I'm glad you're back, Mark."

"I am, too." He was very aware of her soft hand on his neck. Without a doubt, there were certain disadvantages to going to a men's college. "How was college?"

"All right," she said. "You?"

"Okay."

"Have you talked to any of the kids? Everybody's here."

"A few," Mark said. "It's funny. I thought everybody would come back changed, but nobody is, really. Their clothes are just different or their hair is longer or shorter, but they aren't changed."

"I know. What do you think about Jerry Barnhill?"

"It's too bad," Mark said, and that was about all that there was to say, so he didn't say anything more, and she didn't say anything either, and they just went along until finally somebody took off the record or something; anyway, the music stopped. Joan drifted off, and Mark began to wander around the room.

To one side, he found a small knot of boys busy

remembering all the high school football games and baseball games and track meets they had been in. In their midst was Tom Radasch, a tall stocky boy who had been the best athlete in their class. He was speaking as Mark came up.

"And you remember that time when we played Manhasset the second time, away? It was all tied up with thirty seconds to go and we had that big old last second jumper to squeak it out?" He waited for all the nodding heads and laughs of remembrance. "That was the greatest play of all. I got the old apple from half court and I was really shook but I popped it up and snap! It hits the old nets for two as the buzzer sounds." He shook his head, laughing. "What a game. That Emerson almost blocked it, too. Remember Emerson? That blonde kid from Manhasset, played forward? He was on the track team, too. He high jumped. You remember. He did five-nine that time we had a meet in the rain. He was pretty good. But we still won the old meet. That was the day I cleared twenty two feet in the broad jump,

Crichton at age 17, receiving a basketball award

and the Goddam pit was a sandy puddle. What a day." There were more laughs and more talking; Mark drifted off.

Liz came up to him, out of no place in particular. She slapped him in the stomach, and it was a pretty hard slap. Mark was glad he wasn't carrying his drink.

"Hi, Liz. How's Bennington?"

"Great," she said, her long blonde hair swirling as she moved her head. Liz always had had beautiful hair, and she had always been proud of it and kept it long. "Just great. How have you been?"

"Fine."

"Did I tell you I'm glad you didn't go to Williams? I am. The kids at Williams are creeps. But I mean creeps. But I met this kid at a mixer, who is quitting at the end of the term, and he's great. Really cool. You should meet him. You would like him. The only thing is, he lives in Vermont."

Well, Liz hasn't changed, Mark thought. "How is your skiing?"

"Fabulous. Only it should be better. I wanted to go to Stowe this week but my parents wanted me to stay home. Sometimes they give me a hard time. You know parents. But I skied a weekend before I even came home, and it was really good."

"I guess you heard about Jerry."

"Barnhill? Yes, sure. Doesn't it just make you sick, Mark? I mean the whole thing. About dying in a crash and all. It's sickening, any way you look at it. He was so young, he never had a chance to find out what life is all about."

Mark didn't say anything. He wondered if Liz knew how ridiculous she sounded.

"The whole thing just makes me sick all over. It wouldn't be so great to die when you're all old and everything, but it makes me sick to think of dying so soon. And you know what else? Nobody even thinks about him. Nobody at all. He's just dead, so what the hell. Nobody thinks or remembers him. It's just like he never was. Like what Hemingway said in—"

"Oh, come on, Liz."

"But it's true. Nobody went to the funeral."

"Really? I heard there were a lot of people there."

"Oh sure. But not kids. Lots of old people and friends of Mr. Barnhill and of the family. People like that. But not many kids."

"Well, maybe they weren't back for their vacations yet. I wasn't."

"They were back. They just didn't bother to come. I think it's pretty rotten, too. The kids in our class are so rotten, Mark. Look at them now. Do you think they are paying any attention to the fact that Jerry's dead?"

"Yes," Mark said, looking around. "I've heard a lot of people talking about it."

"Oh, sure, talking. Just like they'd talk if the Russians had sent a man to hell. It's just a topic of conversation. But are they paying any attention, really?"

Mark sighed. "What do you want out of them, Liz?"

She frowned. "A little respect, that's all. Just a little respect. Just for a while. Just to be decent about it."

Mark didn't say anything, and Liz took another sip of her drink. "By the way, did I tell you I'm entered in the Sugar Slalom. It's at Mount Mansfield. Last year I finished eleventh. But this year I should do much better."

Mark would have said something, but Liz quickly excused herself and slipped away, into the central tangle of dancers. He turned around, and there was the ubiquitous, smiling Fred Adams.

According to his 👉
high school yearbook,
Crichton was "G.O.
Veep." He was also named
class writer (male) and
among those "most likely
to succeed."

He liked Freddy; back in high school Freddy had been the president of the student council and Mark had been the vice-president. They had worked diligently together for a long and conscientious year as the political leaders of their fair school. And now here was Freddy, his hand stuck out, with his best and most winning smile on. He was wearing a ROTC uniform.

"Hi, Fred," Mark said, taking the hand. "Good to see you. How's school?"

"Good, very good. Couldn't be better." He gave Mark what Mark thought must be Fred's most firm, confident and cordial handshake. "And you?"

"Fine. I see you're in Rotsy."

"Yes, yes," Freddy said, running his hands over his sides, feeling the buttons.

"And I see you're wearing your Rotsy uniform."

"Listen, I *like* this uniform," Freddy said positively. "I think it's sharp. I don't see what's wrong with wearing this uniform. Just because nobody else does doesn't mean it's wrong or something. I think it's a sharp uniform. Why shouldn't I wear it?"

"No reason at all. Free country."

"That's what I say. And our armed services are doing a great service to our country, and it ought to be more grateful. Lots of places, this uniform is a contemptible thing, and it shouldn't be. I think it's cool." He fingered the brass, casually.

Mark nodded, and said nothing.

"Listen," Fred said. "There's been a lot of talk about setting up a scholarship fund in memory of Jerry Barnhill. His family wants to do it, and some people called me up and thought that it would be, you know, nice if our class sort of started it off, since we were in his class and everything. So I'm going to go around to all the parties and see all last year's seniors. Think it's a good idea?"

"Sure."

"Then why don't you start off the contributions? Don't give anything too much so it will look funny. Just—well, you know."

Mark took a dollar out of his wallet and gave it to Freddy. Freddy didn't say a word, but reached into his own wallet and conspicuously took out a five and put it in his hand with Mark's one. He smiled. "Well, I'm off. Wish me luck."

"Good luck."

Mark felt like another drink, and he headed off toward the bar. On the way, he met Mr. Gilbert. Mr. Gilbert was really a pretty good guy, as far as parents went, and he had always been good to Mark all the time he had been taking Joan out.

"Mark my boy! Good to see you again. How's school?"

"Fine. How've things been for you?"

"Very good, as a matter of fact. Can't complain. They working you pretty hard up there?"

"Yes, pretty hard."

"Well, we've all heard that you're doing very well. Say, isn't that thing about the Barnhill boy awful?"

"Yes, it's a real shame."

"I never knew the boy—Jerry, wasn't it?—except by sight. Did you know him?"

"A little."

"Nice boy? Seemed like a nice boy."

"Yes," Mark said. "He was a good guy."

"Well, sooner or later they're going to have to do something about these Goddam airlines, that's all." He shook his head and clicked his tongue. "Well, I'll talk to you later, Mark."

"Right," Mark said, but he was already gone. [. . .]

The author addresses difficulties he had with his own parents in Travels. *In* Jurassic Park *one of Crichton's characters makes an interesting connection between parents and dinosaurs: "children liked dinosaurs because these giant creatures personified the uncontrollable force of looming authority. . . . Fascinating and frightening, like parents."*

THE MOST IMPORTANT PART OF THE LAB

(1 9 6 1 , A G E 1 8)

I ate quickly and headed for the lab right after lunch. It was a clear, windy March afternoon, but not very cold. As I came up Mt. Auburn street, I saw that Elsie's was crammed with wonks, all standing around with their elbows high, munching. They stared out at me through the dirty glass, beneath the neon sign. I walked by quickly.

As I passed Elsie's, I heard someone trip on the brick sidewalk behind me, and then I heard a groan. I looked back without breaking stride, and saw someone lying there, stretched out on the ground. It was a guy, lying half on the pavement, half in the street, and he wasn't moving. I waited for a moment to see if someone nearer the guy would stop and help him, but nobody did, so I went back, and bent over him. People walked by me on both sides, their coats flapping in the wind. They gave me funny looks as they passed, as if I had done something to the guy.

The fellow's eyes were shut; his forehead rested on the edge of the curb, and the skin was split slightly. He was bleeding, but not much. As the people walked by, I caught snatches of conversation over my head.

". . . doesn't have any idea how to run a seminar . . ."

"I don't know why she said it. . ."

The guy was young, an undergraduate. Carefully, I shook him by the shoulder. I felt a little foolish, squatting there in the early afternoon at the corner of Mt. Auburn and Holyoke, shaking some guy lying on the ground.

"Yes, but is it *valid* ?"

". . . never knew he drank until I saw him sober. . ."

People kept looking back at me, but nobody stopped. At knee level, I watched them all hurry by. Somebody kicked my bookbag, but didn't even turn around to see what it was.

The guy didn't move, so I shook him a little harder. I didn't really know what to do. Once, I had taken a first aid course, but I had forgotten it all. I wished somebody would stop, but nobody did. Finally, I grabbed the coat of a professor-type as he went by, and asked him to find a cop. I told him this fellow was hurt. The professor gave me a funny look, and said he would try to find a cop, but he kept right on going and never once looked back.

It was about then that the fellow on the ground opened his eyes. He seemed dazed, and tried to sit up. I helped him. Then the crowd began to gather, and almost immediately a whole group of people was standing around, talking and flapping in the wind. They completely enclosed the two of us, him sitting, and me squatting beside him. A car came past us, and I helped the guy move back, so he wouldn't get hit. I gave him my handkerchief for his cut, which was bleeding more now.

He looked at me. "I'm all right," he said.

"What happened? I heard something, and looked around, and there you were. You've been out for a bit."

"I'm okay now."

"Are you sure?"

"Sure." He began to get up, but I held him down.

"Just wait a minute. Don't rush." I used to faint when I got shots when I was a kid, so I knew he shouldn't get up too soon.

But the guy was looking up at the crowd, towering over us. He seemed embarrassed, and tried to straighten his tie. "I've got to get going."

"Why don't you go over to the Health Center?"

Hammond, Jurassic Park's *loathsome magnate, delivers this business tip: "Personally, I would never help mankind."*

Crichton loves a medical mystery. In The Andromeda Strain, *he clearly enjoys having the scientists puzzle over what exactly has wiped out an entire Arizona town.* ☞

"This section is ☞ slightly more feeble than the rest," suggests Crichton's teacher, referring to the next two paragraphs. "From here on in, it's fine."

"No, really, I'm all right now."

"You probably need stitches," I said. "And you still look pretty pale. What happened? Did you just pass out?"

"Really, I'm fine. I feel fine now. I'll just go eat lunch." He stood up, and so did I. The crowd moved back, murmuring to itself. No one said anything to either of us. I wished again that a cop would come and make the guy go to the Health Center. People don't just pass out in front of Elsie's for no reason.

I looked up toward the Square, hoping to see a cop coming down. There was none around that I could see. When I looked back, the guy was gone. I looked at the crowd, at all the faces, and finally said to some girl with black hair and big eyes, "Where did he go?" She looked at me like I was nuts, to be talking to a total stranger like her. I turned to a man with white hair. "Did you see that fellow that was here a minute ago? Where did he go?" The man shook his head and shrugged.

I looked around once again, and broke out of the crowd. I went around the corner to look down Mt. Auburn Street. He was nowhere in sight. I went back to the crowd, which was still standing in the same spot, talking quietly. Apparently, everyone had forgotten why they had gathered there in the first place.

I remembered my lab, and rummaged around all the legs looking for my bookbag. Above me, the people watched with detached interest. Finally, I found it; a girl with wrinkled stockings and fat ankles was standing on it like it was her pedestal. I tugged at it, but she didn't notice. I asked her to please move, interrupting a conversation she was having with some balding section man. Annoyed, she wordlessly got down off my bookbag. I headed for the lab. I looked back once, and the crowd was still there.

I arrived for the lab two minutes late, and Mr. Hopkins, the lab man, had already begun his little pre-lab talk. When I came in, he gave me his best withering look—he has several grades of them—and I tried to look contrite.

"I was just telling the class, Mr. Gordon, that when you cut down midsection, you must be very careful not to puncture the diaphragm. And you must work quickly. If you are lucky, you may still see the lungs in operation." He turned back to the rest of the class. "If you are not in time, you can still inflate the lungs by cutting through the trachea, inserting an eyedropper, and blowing air into the lungs. After you have observed the lungs, cut the diaphragm and expose the heart." His voice droned on. I opened the lab book and stopped paying attention to him. I noticed vaguely that we were dissecting rats, but my mind was on the guy on Holyoke Street. He really bothered me, and I couldn't help wondering what had happened to him.

Finally, Hopkins stopped talking. He began to inject drugs into the rats, bringing the injected rats around to members of the class. With a sickening smile, he gave me mine first. "I thought you'd like to get an early start," he said. "Just let it run around; it'll collapse in a minute." He paused. "But you will, of course, want to record the effects of the narcotic." I took the rat by its thick tail, and set it down on the desk in front of me. It scurried about for a while; when it began to get away, I would drag it back by the tail. Soon, it began to stagger, and then it sagged, and lay panting on the desk top. Behind me, I could hear Hopkins explaining to some girl that the effects were similar to alcohol in humans. My rat just lay there, spread-eagled on its stomach, panting.

Hopkins finished handing out the rats, and came

An angry dinosaur pursues Grant around a laboratory in Jurassic Park, *until the scientist saves himself by injecting the encroaching beast with a syringe of toxin.*

back to me. "I don't want to belabor this, Mr. Gordon, but you've been late for the last three labs. I'm sure the rest of the class would appreciate your being on time, and avoiding interruptions. It's not that much to ask, you know."

I decided then to explain the whole thing to him. I didn't really care about Hopkins' opinion, only his grade. That was why I told him. Hopkins listened without a word, wearing that flat, pleasant look which was his interpretation of scientific objectivity mixed with humanism. "Well," he said finally, "you've had an interesting day, haven't you?" He looked down at the rat. "I believe you can begin dissection now."

The rat had completely passed; its eyes were shut and its mouth was open. I picked it up carefully, feeling its disturbing warmth, and dropped it into the pan on its back. I pinned its paws down, stretching the fur across its stomach.

People around me had already begun cutting. One fat Cliffie was going at it passionately; her fingers and scissors were all bloody, and, as she bent over the animal, her chubby nose was pleated in reaction to the smell. I adjusted my glasses, stalling, but finally, when I caught another of Hopkins' looks, I had to start. I snipped the rat open, slowly. With each cut, I could feel the texture of the skin and fur.

I cut through the fur, then the muscle, exposing the insides. They were all red, and I drained away some of the blood. I was too late to see the lungs going, so I cut through the diaphragm and looked at the heart. It was small, but still beating. I examined it, but couldn't tell much. It was just a small pulsing spot of red stuff, not very interesting at all. You would have thought a living heart, any heart, would be interesting, but this one wasn't.

As a medical student, ☞ Crichton often met health care professionals who were a bit short on humanism. Like the resident in Travels who would yank at patients in their beds, shouting "No, no, not like that, just stay the way I had you!"

The premed track at ☞ Harvard was "nasty and competitive," writes Crichton in Travels. In his Chem 20 lab, for example, other students would give misinformation "in the hope that you would make a mistake or, even better, start a fire," recalls the author (who started more lab fires that year than anyone else). "I thought that a humane profession like medicine ought to encourage other values in its candidates."

By now, the smell of rat-insides had pervaded the whole lab. Hopkins was gleeful, hopping from desk to desk, glancing from rat to student and back to rat, making infinitely helpful suggestions but never doing any of the work himself. Occasionally, he would stop to address the class as a whole. "Class, class, listen up, please. Cut away each organ and examine it as you go. And be sure to get the whole of the small intestine. You'll need it for the next lab. Work quickly; you mustn't waste your time." He chuckled. "Or the rat's."

All around me, bored students were cutting up their rats, slicing out organs, sticking them under microscopes, drawing pictures. The only interested people seemed to be the ones that enjoyed it. "I wish we didn't have to do rats," someone said. "Frogs are much nicer. I did a frog once in high school and it didn't smell at all."

"It's because they're mammals," explained a Cliffie. It was the one with the braces. "Closer to man and all."

"Hey," shouted a boy in the back. "Mine's pregnant!"

Everyone looked up, and Hopkins scampered over. "Class, I want you all to look at this," he said. "We'll put one of the embryos under the dissecting scope, and be sure you note the embryonic form, and the structures that are developed." He put something under the microscope. "Why, you can even see their little hearts beating," he announced. "Quite remarkable. Be sure you take a look at this."

I worked steadily, fighting my disgust. I had never dissected much of anything before, and I disliked the whole business. Personally, I would rather learn it from books. It seemed a great waste to kill 30 rats for as many students, just so they could cut them open

Ian Malcolm, the mathematician in Jurassic Park, *faults scientific discovery as an "aggressive, penetrative act. . . . Discovery is always a rape of the natural world. Always."*

and take a quick look. After all, you couldn't learn much. Aside from the actual experience, there was very little of value.

At the end, I cut out the small intestine, smelling the stink from the colon. I dropped the intestine into a test tube of preservative and put the remains of the rat into the trashcan. With relief, I washed my hands. Then, remembering the embryos, I went to the scope and drew a quick sketch. It was nearly trans-

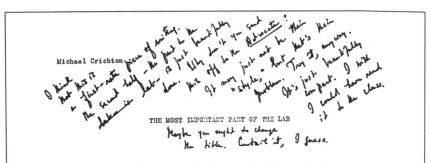

THE MOST IMPORTANT PART OF THE LAB

I ate quickly and headed for lab right after lunch. It was a clear, windy March afternoon, but not very cold. As I came up Mt. Auburn street, I saw that Elsie's was crammed with wonks, all standing around with their elbows high, munching. They stared out at me through the dirty glass, beneath the neon sign . I walked by quickly.

As I passed Elsie's, I heard someone trip on the brick sidewalk behind me, and then I heard a groan. I looked back without breaking stride, and saw someone lying there, stretched out on the ground. It was a guy, lying half on the pavement, half in the street, and he wasn't moving. I waited for a moment to see if someone nearer the guy would stop and help him, but nobody did, so I went back, and bent over him. People walked by me on both sides, their coats flapping in the wind. They gave me funny looks as they passed, as if I had done something to the guy.

The fellow's eyes were shut; his forehead rested on the edge of the curb, and the skin was split slightly. He was bleeding, but not much. As the people walked by, I caught snatches of conversation over my head.

"...doesn't have any idea how to run a seminar..."

"I don't know why she said it..."

The guy was young, an undergraduate. Carefully, I shook him

parent, with a large eye, and a curled body, mostly head. The limbs were just forming, the fingers still webbed. It was an amazing thing to see, but I felt a little sick, and I wanted to get out.

As I prepared to leave, Hopkins clutched at me. "I hope you remembered to save the small intestine. It's very important."

"Right here," I said, displaying the test tube. He looked disappointed.

"Good lad," he said.

As I left, the one slob who lives in Adams and always makes a mess of things was washing his hands, which were covered with blood, bits of fur, and pieces of innard. I walked out of the lab, and only then remembered the guy on the street again.

I walked home the same way I had come, down Holyoke Street, past the faces in Elsie's. There was no indication that anything had happened there earlier in the day. It was time for dinner, but I didn't feel like eating, so I decided to take a walk along the river. I went to the other side; the sun was setting, and it was getting windier. It was actually a little unpleasant, and I did not meet anyone I knew. I was glad. The day had left me depressed, and annoyed with people in general, though I couldn't say exactly why. And that, in itself, was annoying.

Crichton's characters often express irritation or annoyance. Harry Benson in The Terminal Man is visited by a vague, disturbing feeling as one of the electrodes implanted in his brain is tested. "I can't describe it. It's like sandpaper. Irritating."

Michael Crichton

Rita Dove at about age 10

rita dove

M ANY YEARS BEFORE HER book *Thomas and Beulah* won the 1987 Pulitzer Prize for poetry and before she was named—in May 1993—to be the nation's poet laureate, Rita Dove was practicing her art by composing a small verse about a rabbit. "I remember writing 'The Rabbit with the Droopy Ear' during a free-choice period in school; it was near Easter, of course," she recalls. "I was particularly proud of the twist at the end of the poem, especially since I began writing with no idea whatsoever of how the rabbit was going to solve his dilemma."

In her first published novel, *Through the Ivory Gate* (1992), Dove explores childhood creativity. Focusing on a young woman's quest to fulfill her artistic aspirations, *Through the Ivory Gate* is also about coming to terms with youth's confusion and pain. Its protagonist, Virginia King, is a visiting artist-in-the-schools, who is drawn into her students' lives as she strives to inspire their imaginations through puppetry.

Dove, who was born in 1952 in Akron, Ohio, found her own imagination stimulated in grade school, as the excerpts included here from the wonderfully convoluted *Chaos* demonstrate. Written when the author was ten, this twenty-eight-chapter novel was Dove's solution to a vocabulary-building classroom assignment. She explains further:

> *Chaos* was written over the period of one semester. Our fourth-grade teacher allotted approximately twenty-five minutes each Monday afternoon for spelling: we were to acquaint ourselves with the new spelling list and do the exercises in our text. I

would quickly finish the exercises, then write the next chapter of my epic science-fiction saga. The only rules were: (1) each spelling word had to be used in the form presented, (2) the order of the list must be honored, and (3) no peeking at the next week's list. Needless to say, I had no idea what developments in plot or character were going to occur—language was the gondolier, and I was open to adventure. ✐

THE RABBIT WITH
THE DROOPY EAR

The author has re-created this poem from memory.

(CIRCA 1962, AGE 10)

Mr. Rabbit was big and brown,
But he always wore a frown.
He was sad, even though Spring was here,
Because he had one droopy ear.

They were the handsomest ears in town;
'Cept one went up, and one hung down.
And to think Easter was almost here!
Alas for the rabbit with the droopy ear.

The Rabbit went to wise old owl,
And told his tale 'twixt whine and howl.
The owl just leaned closer to hear
And said, "I know the cure for your droopy ear."

In Through the Ivory Gate, *Virginia recalls the childhood desire to fit in. She "knew that gaze well—a child staring into the mirror wondering if she were a freak, gawking at her own eyes staring back."* ☞

The next day everyone gathered 'round to see
The incident at the old oak tree.
Mr. Rabbit hung upside down
From a branch on the tree, and gone was his frown.

Hip, hip hooray—let's toast him a cup,
For now both ears were hanging *up*!
All the animals raised a cheer:
Hooray for the rabbit with the two *straight* ears!

from
CHAOS
(CIRCA 1962, AGE 10)

Chapter II.

The robots had to tackle and tickle the man to make him stumble. The man began to struggle, for he was to smuggle eggs out of the country. As he began to scramble, the eggs became scrambled. It was a horrible sight. The robot was very noble about it, and made it into an article in the Robital Daily. It took up a single column. The robot offered the man a half dollar for an advertisement for a buckle. This was used as an angle. The advertisement was in a triangular shape.

Chapter V.

"The total of 5 and 5 is ten," said the robot student. He was a major in the human brain. He thought, "I will betray myself," for he was a pilot on duty. The mission was beyond and beneath his belief. He smelled bacon, and the odor gave him a fever. Suddenly he felt evil, and could not digest his desire, crazy and severe as it was, to erase the word "unite" on his paper. But all this is past, and we passed on.

Chapter VII.

It was a gloomy and weary day. The rain was steady and dreary. The robot had a fancy that he heard a stingy but dainty lady, but it was too foggy to see the greedy maid. She was a hearty woman, and she promised to identify any envy in a person. But just then, the levy broke, washing several houses away. The lady said, "Now we can modify this neighborhood and the houses will occupy less space. Let's notify the architects and have them apply for the

The author has selected eleven complete chapters for inclusion here. Chapter 1, she says, does not contain any information useful to understanding those that follow.

The reader may confidently deduce that similar words in close proximity to one another came from the 🖎 spelling lessons' lists.

In Through the Ivory Gate, teenage Virginia discovers the downside to a superior vocabulary when she scares off one potential boyfriend unfamiliar with the word exempt. "'It sounds like a very useful word,'" he says, after her self-conscious explanation. "'Thank you for the lesson.'"

jobs." The robot thought his actions were justified. He said, "Isn't this weather nice?" She laughed and walked into the fog. Whether she heard him or not, no one knows.

Chapter VIII.

"The cat is in the pantry!" she cried. The robot answered, "Don't give him any mercy!" Then, on second thought, he added, "Sign a treaty with him and maybe you shall have the victory." He was playing with a battery, while saying, "Honesty is the best Policy." He had a salary to watch over the women, and he had a theory that if he made an inquiry as to what variety of oil he had, she would say "Petroleum." He hated petroleum. It was a mystery, since her amount of property got her in high society. The majority of her clan grabbed at opportunity and a dull personality. It's the quality, not the quantity; the ability, not the activity. As a principal once said, "It's the principle of the thing, not the outcome."

"How could ☞ someone mix up the animal deer *with the salutation* dear*?" wonders Virginia over a suitor's poorly spelled love note in* Through the Ivory Gate. *"Children memorized that rule in third grade."*

Chapter IX.

The rocket ship named *Vanish* was receiving a second coat of varnish. A robot had to punish a boy who had gone to publish the news about the ship. The boy had to furnish enough guns to astonish the people. Another robot went to establish a launching pad, and accomplished it. When the rocket began to operate, the people began to debate as to whether a graduate should ride. One robot made an estimate and decided to cultivate a garden, investigate it to find the astronaut, and congratulate him. He began to organize a searching party, and realized he would have to civilize the members before they could recognize a man. When asked how to choose an astronaut, he said, "I did the choosing, and I chose a man who was the best to be chosen."

Chapter X.

It is legal to get a mental case and make him the country's ideal. Seymour, the robot, thought it natural to create a Paris original and to be loyal to it. He was the local doctor, he gave all physical tests, and was practical about it. He made an electrical maid who was very dismal. She turned into a criminal and looked comical. The actual maid was official. There was a similar case to this, which is very peculiar. A very popular man saw a face familiar to his. He has been more particular than his twin since then.

Chapter XIV.

The lawyer made an action against the robot who took a portion of a pie, not to mention a position in the air force. The solution seemed to be to find the location of this robot so keen on aviation. The situation had a solid foundation and an operation had to be performed by a doctor of that occupation (aviation), to solve it. The doctor's imagination was great, and his idea of civilization was a sort of organization.

Rita Dove at right (about age 10), with siblings
Ray and Robin

He had a mansion and was on a mission. He has a pension and hated religion. His opinion of fashion was "stupid!" He liked to write but wasn't a writer. When he puts his words in writing, wise ones are written.

Chapter XXIII.

The robot made a wreck out of the wreath when he began to wrestle with a sword. He bumped against a door knob, and knit his brows in concentration. He used his knowledge to judge whether he should go to the lodge that night. His mind was filled with doubt, and he realized he was in debt. But the robot was calm, and began to study his palm, from which a corn stalk had grown. He had salmon for supper and a cake prepared from scratch. Then, with a sign, he arose and began to design a type of freight train, used to carry foreign goods. As he read a newspaper column on the subject, he thought, "I plan to have planned this train by tomorrow, so I better start planning."

Chapter XXIV.

Rita Dove

With a rope around his waist, Seymour the robot began to sow the ground on his farm. He wished for a soul, but kept tight reins on Knight, the old plow horse who was born on a pier while his mother waited for a ferry boat. He felt like he was dying, but of course he wasn't due for his annual oil checks. Seymour also wished for laws, and he worshipped a straw idol. The border of his farm and his sneaky neighbor, Malkolk, was a river with a big mouth bass in it. Malkolk had found a vein of gold near the river, the color of an egg yolk. With the money he decided to marry a robot who was a bore. He was halfway up the aisle when a colonel rushed in with a council behind him. He said, "I will try to tell you, but I need many tries." What he had tried to say was that the gold was Seymour's and he had been trying to stop the wedding.

Chapter XXVI.

A robot college student was to diagram the principles of democracy for a biography of a man interested in photographs. This was his project for his senior year. He also wrote a paragraph about an amphibian he had seen through a telescope. When he sent the beast a telegram written by a stenographer, the beast looked at it under a microscope and said there was a germ on it. The thermometer read 100°, and the beast, which was a dinosaur, began to look at a cloth catalogue. The college student also studied chemistry at an academy. His motto: "long after the dinosaur becomes a skeleton, someone will look over the horizon and wonder about a planet like ours. During this period, cameras inside a satellite will be busy, taking pictures of space. Remember, when one busies oneself, he appears busied, and usually means business."

Puppets, rather than robots, act out the imaginative impulses of Virginia's grade-schoolers in Through the Ivory Gate. *"Puppets don't have the limitations of human beings. . . . They are free from any real feeling. They are indestructible, even immortal . . . ," says Virginia, explaining children's attraction to these surrogates. "Put a puppet into a child's hands and she knows all these things instinctively."*

Chapter XXVIII.

The human cowboy was singing a solo while riding a bucking bronco. He was an alto, but could sing soprano. He came to a deserted pueblo village and captured a burro. He radioed into the president, who vetoed the idea of issuing an embargo to the robots. When the cowboy yelled hello to a cliff, an echo came back. He looked up at the cliff and saw a robot eating a tomato sandwich and potato sticks. His motto was, "A buffalo can't kill a mosquito, but our cargo yesterday was late." A volcano in Honduras coughed, and the hobo in New Jersey found a domino. But the cowboy had given up banjo lessons in order to find his lasso. His success in finding this necessary equipment was a definite disappointment.

Clyde Edgerton at age 15

clyde edgerton

L IKE THE BUZZARD WHO narrates the first piece that follows, Clyde Edgerton has enjoyed a bird's-eye view of his native North Carolina. An Air Force pilot who served in Southeast Asia in 1970 and 1971, Edgerton flew his own plane—a 1946 Piper PA-12 Super Cruiser— above the Tarheel State until a recent accident grounded the craft.

Born in 1944 near Chapel Hill, where he lives today, the author of *Raney* (1985), *Walking Across Egypt* (1987), *The Floatplane Notebooks* (1988), and *Where Trouble Sleeps* (1997), specializes in warmly humorous chronicles of southern life, replete with fried okra and homespun folk tunes. His characters are generally good-hearted—some of them slightly wayward, or poignantly ingenuous—as they concern themselves with, among other things, how to be good Christians in their own highly varied circumstances. Occasionally they are the objects of pointed satire, though more often Edgerton lets them off easy with some good-natured ribbing, the kind he is practicing below on his schoolmates and on himself.

The author sets up his juvenilia:

> When I was fifteen, a sophomore at Southern High in Durham, North Carolina, two friends and I got lost in the woods behind the school one day. My English teacher, Linda Hunt, asked me to write about the experience for the school newspaper, *The Southern Script*. I had never written for publication and I did not consider using my real name. . . .

The following year, Mrs. Hunt asked me to write a piece on basketball practice for the school's literary magazine, *The Southern Drawl.* I complied.

It is clear to me that the "new journalism" of the late '60s (Wolfe, et al.) sprang from these two pieces. ✍

BUZZARD GETS BIRD'S-EYE VIEW OF THREE-MAN ADVENTURES

*Chick, Clyde, Burton Lose Themselves
in True Woodsman Style*

(1960, AGE 15)

I'm a buzzard and not very used to writing for newspapers, but what I'm going to write I figured was good enough to write so I decided to write about it. Well, anyway, while I was floating around over your high school the other day, I noticed three suspicious-looking characters venturing away from a group of students on a field trip (it was one of Miss Honeycutt's classes if I'm not mistaken). From what I could hear I learned that the three boys were Chick, Clyde, and Burton and were on a great adventure to free a poor little crawfish from a cooped-in fishbowl. They traveled down Cook Road for a way and then down a bank by a bridge to a creek. With tearful goodbyes from our three explorers the crawfish was freed into cool, calm waters.

While standing there watching the crawfish slowly swim away, Clyde said, "Boys, I think we'd better hurry back. You know what Miss Honeycutt said!"

"We could take a short cut across the creek, and through the woods and come out right behind the school," Burton replied.

The one called Chick, who looked to be about three feet eight inches tall and weighed about seventy-five pounds said, "Second the motion."

Well, I didn't think they were ever going to find a place to cross the creek. But finally a rather narrow place came up, and after a heated argument over whether to wade, jump, swim, or build a boat and paddle across, they decided to jump. After the three jumped, it ended up Burton, being dry as a match, Chick the same, and Clyde as wet as a drowned rat. After a few laughs Burton started singing "Davy Crockett" and the boys started walking in the direction in which they thought the school would be. Well, folks, they walked and they walked and they walked, and then walked some more. After a while they stopped in a little opening and looked at each other real funny like.

Chick looked up at his comrades and said, "Boys, I think we're lost."

In unison Clyde and Burton replied, "Me too."

With an air of authority Chick calmly stated, "Now let's figure this thing out, boys."

So they commenced to figure things out. They decided to decide in which direction the sun set and at the same time imagine how they were sitting in sixth period, and then they could add things together and come to the conclusion of where the school was.

Chick said, "Now, let's see, where does the sun set?"

Instantly the three woodsmen pointed in three different directions. From my position I could see that Burton was pointing east; Clyde, South, and Chick declared that if the sun didn't set in the north he would eat every tree in sight.

Edgerton chooses an even less expected narrator for part of The Floatplane Notebooks: *a wisteria vine, which, like the buzzard, serves to observe human activity from a certain remove.*

After considerable mumblings, pointings, etc., they started off again, this time running, hoping to come out at any familiar place. In about five minutes they stopped again, out of breath. It was decided that somebody was going to have to climb a tree and see if he could see the school, and instantly four eyes were upon Chick.

A tall, sturdy tree was found. But there was one small problem—how to reach that first limb which was a pretty good way up the trunk. But after about fourteen tries the point of destination was reached.

In his wee, squeaky voice Chick said, "I (pause) think (pause) this limb's (pause) gonna break."

"Pull up, crazy," came an order from below.

About that time there was a loud crash and down came the limb, Chick and all. A footprint was planted on Clyde's shoulder and another directly above his left ear. With three thuds Chick hit the ground (he bounced three times) and got up with a groan. While all this was going on Burton was leaning against a tree holding his stomach with laughter.

After the Jungle Jims stalked through the wild for a while more, having no idea where they were, they came to a place where a road was being built through the woods. A spark of hope came and the boys began walking down the road, hoping to come out somewhere where there was a sign of civilization.

"Boys, if we come in all clean and tell 'em we got lost they won't believe us. I think we ought to walk through a little mud," said Clyde (his clothes were dry by this time).

"You first," said Burton.

But it was too late. Clyde had sneaked around behind him and given him a push into a nice mud puddle. Then the chase was on, Burton after Clyde. About the time Burton caught up with Clyde a mush, muddy, gushy place in the road was reached.

Still partial to the drama of a character out on a limb, Edgerton has Robert cling to a rotten ladder in Walking Across Egypt *and Wesley hang from a sagging house gutter in* Killer Diller. *Like Chick here, they both fall—to great comic effect.* ☞

All at the same time Clyde slipped, grabbed Burton, and started miring up in the mush. There was no refuge for Burton but Clyde's back, so upon it he went and Clyde was in mud well over his sock tops.

After things settled down it was discovered that Clyde had lost a shoe in the mud. It was quite a sight to see him fishing in the muck for it, while Burton and Chick were sitting on a stump laughing heartily.

Many more steps were taken but soon the boys came up behind the school and I expect they felt about like Balboa when he saw the Pacific.

The last time I saw them they were entering one of the back doors of your building. I don't know what happened after that, and if you wish to know, I guess you'll have to ask one of the Three Musketeers.

—Buzzy

At his English teacher's request, the author illustrated his own text

AN AFTERNOON
IN THE GYM

by Gym Mouse

(1960, AGE 16)

To begin the typical day of practice, Steve Utley has the team to sit quietly around the dressing room while he reads his many love letters from all over the United States (especially Washington). Then while everyone is getting into his gym suit, we see Floyd Couch standing in front of the mirror flexing his muscles and admiring the handsome young fellow he sees before him.

Being fully dressed, everyone heads for the gym. John Wheeler rushes through the gym doors, trips over a floor mop, falls onto a ping pong table, and gets things started off with a bang.

Next the terrible task of mopping the gym floor now stands before the players. Floyd Couch and Crawford Williams volunteer. These two young men will not turn down the call of duty. So striking in there like brothers, they fight through the dust and have the floor spick and span in three minutes flat.

Now everyone must do at least fifteen or twenty push-ups. And we see the president of the student body, good 'ole honest-faced Eddie Tice (who is captain of the team, and should set an example) sneak over into a corner and do exactly three and one half push-ups.

Well, after push-ups comes the task of jumping rope. Tyree McGhee and John Whitley have a considerable amount of trouble getting the rope over the top of their heads. Perhaps some day ropes long enough for them will be found.

A few more exercises are performed and then a commotion is heard at the door and in rushes Dan

Clyde Edgerton

Hill and Danny Walker, about an hour late. They were sure that the Varsity practiced last, so they had gone shopping. Wonder what for?

Now is the time for lay-ups and Tyree McGhee gets his ear hung in the net. Woolard Lumley and Crafton Mitchell rush in with the first aid kit. During the rescue job, these two swell managers, armed with scissors, manage to give Ty a nice haircut and cut off three-fourths of his left ear (swell managers?).

After lay-ups the team goes through a few plays during which Lawson Baker springs his little finger and lays out of practice for the next two weeks. You know, it hurts when he runs.

To complete practice, the team usually runs from twenty to thirty laps (John Wheeler never runs over twelve) and then heads for the showers.

Everyone realizes, I'm sure, that there are certain trouble makers on every team. And there is true evidence of this after practice. The well behaved boys such as Garwood House, John Wheeler, Dan Hill, Clyde Edgerton, and Danny Walker have a very hard time enduring the misbehaving and unruly frolicking of Eddie Tice, Crawford Williams, Mike Knowles and a few other naughty ones. These inconsiderate boys always manage to leave the locker room in complete turmoil, while the well-behaved boys I spoke of before reserve all of the blame and have to clean up the mess.

Thus endeth another day of practice.

Everyone retires to Hill's Brown Bomber, Crawford's Grey Ghost, Edgerton's Blue Bullet, or Mitchell's Green Dragon and heads for home leaving John Whitley lingering behind saying, "See 'ya tomorrow, coach."

☛ The adult Edgerton continues to get laughs out of sports-and-cartilage mishaps. Raney's kid brother ends up with a miscast "fish hook hung in his nose."

He's one of the least of these my brethren," says Wesley, inserting a bit of biblical phrasing into a casual conversation. The misfit protagonist of Killer Diller *is preoccupied with the Bible. Like other Edgerton characters, he reads it often, refers to it, and argues ☛ its meanings.*

Gail Godwin at age 14 or 15

gail godwin

AFTER HER PARENTS SEPARATED, when she was two, Gail Godwin lived with her grandmother and mother, who supported the three of them in part by writing pulp romance stories. In her autobiographical essay "Becoming a Writer" (1979), Godwin says that her father was absent from her life for so long that she didn't recognize him when he showed up at her high school graduation. Three years later he committed suicide.

Best known for her novels, including *A Mother and Two Daughters* (1982), *Father Melancholy's Daughter* (1991), and *Evensong* (1999), Godwin is especially attuned to the tides and turbulence of families. In prose fluent in the languages of emotion, psychology, and spirituality, her works often describe her characters' efforts to understand and rise above childhood pain—especially when it involves a missing parent.

Born in Birmingham, Alabama, in 1937, Godwin grew up in North Carolina. She wanted to be a writer from the age of five and began composing short stories four years later.

"The Choice," written when Godwin was fourteen, prefigures elements of her 1985 novel *The Finishing School*, in which a fourteen-year-old girl searches for the path that will make her most alive. And *A Southern Family* (1987) refers on numerous occasions to the Catholic school that so shaped the novel's protagonists, albeit in ways more various and subtle than Godwin's juvenile short story "The Accomplice" would suggest.

Looking back at her file of juvenilia, Godwin observes in a 1987 essay: "What is interesting is that, though the writing has improved, the old themes haven't changed very much." Society's pressure on the individual, life choices, ambition and thwarted ambition are among the key issues that have followed Godwin through the years.

"Each of these childhood concerns," writes Jane Hill in her 1992 critical study of the author, "finds its way into almost every story and novel Godwin has written as an adult." ✍

THE ACCOMPLICE
(1951, AGE 14)

In A Southern Family, Thalia remembers sending her daughter to Catholic high school: "'It cost more, but I'm sure glad we did it. . . . There was this nun there that sure did straighten her out.'" ☞

Nancy had feared Mother Blanche ever since that awful fall day when Mother and Daddy had deposited her at St. Catherine's. The huge nun had glared down on Nancy with unwavering intensity and Nancy had felt that her whole appearance was dreadfully offensive and hastened to bend down and tug at a knee sock and pat the heavy pigtails in order to correct some of the offensiveness.

Mother Blanche had icy eyes which were the shape and color of granite slabs. Her body was obscured beneath the heavy black folds of her garments, and only her terrible red face could be seen peering through the frame of the stiff white bonnet.

"We shall see that Nancy gets the proper discipline and training while she is at St. Catherine's," she boomed to Nancy's parents. "And of course all our students from the first grade up are required to learn French and to speak it during all recitations. We are, as you probably know, a French order."

Nancy noticed that Mother Blanche had not fawned or fumbled with her fingers as Miss Rippy the first grade teacher at P.S. 88 had always done in the presence of parents.

And ever since that first day Nancy had been haunted by the possibility that she might sink further into disfavor with Mother Blanche.

When she heard the familiar thudding walk on the dormitory halls late at night, when she saw the nun thundering across the wooden-floored assembly room to call roll before morning prayers, when she looked out the window and spied her crunching angrily through the helpless autumn leaves on the way back from the chapel, Nancy always went over the whole day in her mind and tried to think if she had done anything wrong. Every time Mother Blanche came in Nancy's direction, she was sure that she had done something that she shouldn't have.

Some of the other second-graders had whispered to Nancy that Mother Blanche had two extra eyes in the back of her head and that even when she appeared to have her back to you she was really just watching you out of those other eyes which were hidden cleverly behind the crisp black veil. "That way, she can catch you doing things better," they informed their terrified new classmate.

And then Nancy had been caught talking to Barbara Van Amm, the girl in front of her, as the class marched in from recess. She had been telling Barbara about how the other school had been last year and how the teachers were just ordinary people who wore dresses and skirts and things. Nancy knew you weren't supposed to talk in line, but she had not been talking very loud. Nobody could have possibly heard her. But Mother Blanche of the four eyes and the supersensitive hearing had heard. She suddenly halted at the head of the line. She turned and snatched her silver whistle which hung from a chain around her neck; she blew the whistle, and then faced Nancy with a face made redder by the effort of blowing the whistle.

After Ralph, A Southern Family's patriarch, tells an off-color joke about a nun, Julia finds the laughter to be forced. "Julia and every one of Lily's children had gone to St. Clothilde's . . . , and images of real nuns, particular nuns, were rising reproachfully in each of their ❧ memories. . . ."

"You there! You were talking in line," she announced dolefully.

The whole line seemed to shrink back. Only Nancy was left to face the large black opponent. She looked desperately down at her dusty red loafers and had the absurd thought that the dust would not come off and she would have to get another pair of shoes.

"No recess for you tomorrow, Lady Chatterbox. You will sit in the summerhouse and write your French verbs." And the huge nun swung around and resumed her striding leadership at the head of the silent line. The children marched stiffly and obediently into the classroom, some turning furtively to give Nancy a curious look, and the crisis was over. But not the fear which now mushroomed into gigantic proportions within Nancy's heart.

Trudy Callahan tried to explain all about nuns to Nancy: "You non-Catholics have a hard time understanding the sisters because your churches don't have any. But don't feel bad. A lot of the kids that come here to board don't know any more than you do. They're 'prodahstunt' like you. St. Catherine's has lots of 'prodahstunts' because their parents realize that it's a very good school."

St. Clothilde's was "the place in town to go" in A Southern Family, *regardless of the child's religious affiliation.* ☞

Nancy said yes she knew that, because Mamma had SAID they would make her a lady at St. Catherine's, or else . . .

"Well, anyway, as I was telling you—about the nuns," Trudy continued instructively, "they give up their lives to Jesus and never get married and shave off all their hair and devote their lives to praying and teaching us."

"But why?" Nancy wanted to know. "Does Jesus ask them to do it?" Nancy knew all about Jesus. The nuns loved to talk about him. The whole upstairs parlor, where the nuns sat and talked and saw visiting parents was filled with pictures and statues of him. And he was all over the chapel. Especially in front of the altar where old Father Murphy spoke in Latin before breakfast. Jesus was up there too, only this time he was almost naked and he was stretched out on that cross. Nancy could never understand how he could look so calm with all those nails stuck in him.

"No, silly," said Trudy in a patronizing tone. "But they KNOW he wants them to become nuns. Because they have grace and they love him very much."

"Do you think Mother Blanche loves him? How could she love anybody? She screams at everybody."

"Oh, yes. She loves him." Trudy was sure. "She's always going to chapel to visit him. Remember how many times we see her going from the window?"

Nancy said she remembered.

"And you should see when she prays. I watched her once, you know, at vespers when we kneel right behind her, and do you know I looked at the side of her face and it was so peaceful and it wasn't hardly red."

Nancy concluded that Mother Blanche must really love Jesus if he had this effect on her. She was sure now that Mother Blanche would never roar at Jesus.

She decided to investigate and find out more about him. Wouldn't it be wonderful to be someone who did not worry about getting on the wrong side of Mother Blanche!

At table that evening, she asked Mother Mouquet about him. The old nun seemed very pleased and wiped the tiny grease smudges out of the wrinkled corners of her mouth with her napkin and settled back in her chair and told Nancy about him.

"He is the Lord," she began slowly in her broken accent. Nancy had to bend towards Mother Mouquet to understand her.

In her October 8, 1982, diary entry about visiting her old convent school, Godwin is flooded with a sense of feeling "thirteen again." It is a sentiment she will draw on in A Southern Family *when* Clare, *on a visit home, feels as though she has never left. "It was as if, after all, the core of her had never escaped, never traveled . . . or written and published books; this part of her remained forever stuck in the nightmare of adolescence. . . ."*

In A Southern Family, *Mother von Blücher "was famous for her ill temper. 'Boy, she really* hates *us!' the little girls would exclaim, fascinated by her perpetual wrath."*

"He was sent here to take away all the bad things that people on earth had done. He was crucified for our sins."

"Why does he make people respect him so?" Nancy wanted to know.

"Oh!" The old nun's eyes brightened, then narrowed. "Because he punishes those who do not respect his laws." She patted Nancy's arm. "It is always a good idea to stay on the right side of the Lord, my little one."

"But what kind of laws did he make?" Nancy demanded eagerly. She had broken enough laws at St. Catherine's already. She hoped there would not be too many more.

Gail Godwin at age 14 or 15

"Love him, love your neighbor, that is enough for you to remember. Just think before you do anything: 'whatever I do to my neighbor, I do to him.' If I hurt my neighbor, I am also hurting him."

"That's one of the rules?"

"That *is* the rule. Woe unto the person who does not treat his neighbor as he would treat Jesus himself." She shook her bony finger at Nancy and Nancy shuddered.

Nancy had lain wide-eyed for what seemed an hour before "lights out" that night. Finally, just before sleep threatened to close in, she figured something out that she had not known before. It concerned Mother Blanche. Mother Blanche was not obeying the law. If she went around shouting and frightening people and not loving them like she did, then she was doing the exact same things to Jesus. Mother Mouquet had been very clear about this law.

She groped around under her pillow until she found the plastic cross that all the boarders got when they came to St. Catherine's. You kept it under your pillow and Jesus was with you all night to guard you from unpleasant things.

There was a moon tonight and some of its thin light seeped into the dark room where Nancy and two other boarders slept. She held the cross in the small square of moonlight on her bedspread. There was just enough light to see the figure. She felt the carved outline with her fingers and wished that she could pull out some of those awful nails.

It was then she decided to make the pact. "Don't worry, Jesus. It's going to be all right. We'll give her one more chance."

She put the cross back under her pillow and fell asleep.

*   *   *   *

Mother Blanche simmered down remarkably the next day. Nancy was not sure if it were just a coincidence or whether Jesus had warned her. But she had not fussed at anyone for loitering in assembly that morning; she had not punished Barbara Van Amm for coloring the pictures of *le cheval* and *la salle á manger* in her book before she knew how to pronounce them. And at recess when Nancy sat penitently in the summer house listening to the playing sounds of the other second graders on the playground below and writing in her best Palmer method handwriting "je suis, vous êtes, il est, elle est. . ." Mother Blanche had strode regally up from the playground and said, "Nancy, you accepted your punishment admirably." Nancy could smell the starchy black habit and the faint odor of soap which always clung to Mother Blanche's body. She almost hoped that Mother Blanche would get through the day.

But doom struck in the form of the boarders' Friday night movie. Every Friday night, all the boarders from grades one through eight would assemble in the small auditorium for a movie. The movies were old ones, because Nancy had seen some of them

Gretchen, the searching young writer in Godwin's 1972 story "Some Side Effects of Time Travel," recalls falling in love at age 12 with Mother Maloney, a 39-year-old convent school nun. During the Friday evening movies they would sit together, "and when the lights went out they held hands in one of the deep pockets of Mother Maloney's habit."

with her parents before she came to St. Catherine's. The man who showed them worked in the projection room of one of the theaters in the city. He was a Catholic, Trudy told her, and offered Friday nights up to God for good works.

The movie was about an old general who had come home from the war. It was in black and white and, although some of the seventh and eighth graders laughed once in awhile, Nancy thought it was very boring. She shifted restlessly in her folding chair which squeaked loudly every time she moved. She bit her fingernails. She looked around at all the other boarders and at the nuns. Some of the younger boarders had dropped their heads and closed their eyes. Others lolled listlessly in the uncomfortable seats. Some of the nuns watched the movie as if they were mildly interested. Old Mother Mouquet was sitting on the back row saying her rosary with her eyes closed. Nancy felt close to the wrinkled old nun who had explained everything last night. Neither of them thought the movie was any good at all.

It was finally over. The lights went on and all the boarders had to file past Mr. O'Keefe who was rewinding the movie and say: "Thank you, Mr. O'Keefe." Nancy's eyes felt gritty and the new light made her squint. There had only been one part of the movie she had liked. That was when the old general ran madly up the winding stairs and yelled to the top of his lungs: "CHARGE!" Several of the sleepy boarders had looked up and laughed. Nancy had thought it was extremely funny. Even Mother Blanche had chuckled. Nancy had heard her all the way across the darkened room.

As the boarders mounted the stairs to their rooms for the night, some of them started talking about how funny the general was, running up the stairs and yelling like that.

"Even Mother Blanche laughed," said Trudy to Nancy.

"I dare somebody to rush up these stairs like he did and yell Charge," challenged one of the older boarders with a malicious gleam in her eyes.

Barbara Van Amm, who never did anything outstanding, pretended to yell. "Charge!" she whispered, brandishing an imaginary sword as the general had done with his.

And then Nancy saw her moment to forever become Mother Blanche's friend. No longer would she have to be scared of the wrathful nun. Nancy would re-enact the general's scene and make Mother Blanche laugh again.

The red face appeared on the landing below Nancy. This was it. Pushing past the boarders in front of her, she raged fiercely up the last flight of stairs. She raised her sword.

"CHARGE!" She screamed magnificently.

The silence was deafening. Nobody laughed. Nancy's echo encored her scene. Mother Blanche turned white and then slowly the red reappeared, deepening in color this time. Fire blazed in the colorless eyes.

She swept back her sash, picked up her long black skirts and made her frightful ascension up the steps until she reached Nancy's level and towered over her.

"It seems," she began, pronouncing each word meticulously, "That some people around here have a flair for creating disturbances. If you are so fond of the summerhouse, Nancy we shall see about letting you sit there every day. But in order to impress it upon you that we do not shout out to the top of our lungs at this hour of the night—"

Several of the nuns who had not gone to the movies stuck their heads out of doors up and down

Julia, in A Southern Family, *once wrote sassy "jump-rope chants" at convent school, "until Mother von Blücher had overheard one and she'd almost been expelled.* (Skinny Vinnie got the minnie, *it had gone. Raged and screamed and cried. / She flushed and flashed / Then trickled and pickled / Until she got* 🐟 *so mad she died.)"*

the hall at the top of the steps. They had taken their veils off, and all that remained on their mysterious heads was a stiff, white covering. Nancy thought of white mice peeking out of their holes.

"In order to impress it upon you that you have created a disturbance," continued the terrible one, "No movie will be shown at all next Friday night. This is your fault, and the girls will obviously not be pleased with you for it."

She closed her mouth as abruptly as a snapping turtle. Her eyes were cold and dangerous like a pond frozen over with thin ice. "March to your rooms." That was all.

The boarders grumbled under their breaths as they resumed their climb. A few of the seventh and eighth graders passed Nancy and muttered rude things without looking at her. One of them was the boarder who had suggested the whole thing in the first place. Trudy said sadly, "Aw, Nancy. What didja do *that* for?"

Nancy undressed quickly while her two room-mates went into the bathroom with their tooth-brushes to talk about her. When they came out, she was already balled up under the blanket, clutching the cross with both hands. They knelt by the side of the bed and executed a rapid "Hailmery." Then the lights went out, and Nancy heard the familiar "clomp, clomp" of the heavy heels grow closer to the door, then pass, and recede into the farthest corner of the hall where—as Nancy knew—*she* slept.

"That's the last time she will ever walk down this hall," Nancy said, stroking the cross. "We certainly did give her a fair chance." She placed the object against her cheek. It was cool and comforting.

She was running, running because she had to get there before it was light. She ran up to the altar, pushing past a silent Father Murphy who was deep in prayer and did not notice her. She stood on tiptoe and pulled with all her strength until, one by one, the nails fell on the floor. And then she took him by the hand, and covered him with the bathrobe she had brought him because it was chilly in the early mornings before it got light. Together, they stole out of the chapel past Father Murphy who still did not look up but acted as if he were in some sort of a trance. Across the hard ground where most of the leaves had been pulverized into dirt by now, and up the stairs and back down the hall, only this time further. And then they opened the door and stood before her—a monstrous mound of blanket with only a little white head covering sticking out from the end. He raised his hand and made magic motions in the air like Father Murphy sometimes did. And it was over. She was finished. As they ran back to the chapel, it was getting light and Nancy wondered how she would look when they found her huge, still form in the morning. They were running, running and then he started pulling her, pulling and jerking her until her whole body jolted and lunged.

She looked through the clumps of sleep-grit clustered in the corners of her eyes. She was being shaken by the shoulders by a figure whose hulking shadow obliterated the window, shutting out all of the morning sunlight, except for a thin line of light which haloed the black head.

"Nancy!" boomed Mother Blanche. "You have overslept and missed morning prayers."

Godwin's fiction pays much attention to dreams. In Father Melancholy's Daughter, *Margaret is abruptly awakened from one by her father, the rector of St. Cuthbert's. He tells her that in the night vandals had sawed down the church's street-corner crucifix.*

THE CHOICE

The township of
Clove, N.Y., in The
Finishing School, ☞
is a similarly insulated
place, where teenage
Justin is trying to discover
her own specialness.

The placid little village of Sunny Bay was for the first time in a state of uproar. During these last few days everybody had been scrambling about in a mad rush to go nowhere. Lately there was an air of importance in this humble habitat. The whole thing could be traced back to the day Lucille LaRose had decided she was bored with being called the "Torrid Lover with the Velvet Lips", tired of the city lights and night clubs, and just plain sick of hundreds of adoring beaus and boxes of a dozen red roses. It was then Lovely Lucile had decided to grace her home town of Sunny Bay as a sort of game.

Mayor McCraw had been wired, (incidentally it was the first telegram he had ever received in his life) and pictures of Lucile were immediately tacked

Gail Godwin at age 19 or 20

up on every billboard and telephone pole within ten miles of Sunny Bay. The villagers were attacked with house-cleaning-itus and the modest little cottages brightened up with enthusiasm. Their windows were washed so clean they outdid the scrubbed flawless complexion of a child. Sunny Bay awaited the one and only thing they could boast about.

Most eager of all the villagers was Sally McCraw, the mayor's daughter. The fourteen year old brown eyed dreamer had been faithfully saving her allowance for three weeks so she could pay the admission necessary to feast one's eyes on Lovely Lucile.

Now on the long awaited day Sally counted her nickels and dimes. By sacrificing love magazines and skipping Neptune Bars, her favorite food, she had somehow managed to scrape up enough to give her seventy-five cents which seemed like chicken feed after all her efforts. Anyway she had just enough.

Miss La Rose was to appear at Town Hall since Sunny Bay did not own a theater. The appearance was scheduled for ten o'clock. However, Sally McCraw was going to take no chances and set out an hour early so she would be sure to get a seat.

The morning felt warm and comfortable and the rays gave Sally a feeling of being half in a dream. She took the Old Harbor Road and lingered as she came to the Bay. The water sparkled so that she blinked once or twice and the shimmering ripples wiggled and flashed like the lights in a big city night. . . . . Madame McCraw leaning on the arm of a luscious Latin American with a moustache stepped from her red sedan. The crowds roared as she nodded and lifted her dainty hand in acknowledgement of the praise and yells. She held the graceful folds of a net dress in her other hand. . . . . Sally walked fast yet she was somewhat astonished when she found herself in front of Mr. Stringer's hardware store. It was only a matter of a few blocks now. She wondered if she were too early.

A sign in the local drugstore caught her eye and her heart did a handspring. The sign said, "Be Lucile Lovely with ENCHANTMENT Facial Soap." Underneath was a very flattering picture of Lucile La Rose herself rubbing up a lather of ENCHANTMENT on her delicate face.

Now Sally was somewhat upset. She had saved faithfully to see Lucile La Rose and dreamed about it many times. She would get to shake the star's hand and might be lucky enough to receive a 10 x 12 autographed picture of Lucile suitable for framing.

Yet suddenly she lost some of her enthusiasm. She gazed at the soap ad and then at her own reflection in the plate glass window. She could either see the star or buy the soap. If she bought the soap she would not have enough money left to get into Town Hall.

The clock in Tom's Jewelry Store told Sally she had better hustle. The soap ad in the window beckoned her. Villagers swarmed into Town Hall two blocks away. Pretty soon the crowd would roar applause and Lucile La Rose would step out of her automobile.

Sally wanted to be able to tell her grandchildren she had shaken hands with the most glamorous star of her day. Yet would it be worth it to spend the rest of her life remembering she had actually touched the star? She liked the thought of Latin American Lovers and red sedans. If she bought the soap she

Nora, the writer ☞ character in Godwin's "Notes for a Story" (1976), recalls writing "The Magic Lipstick" as a child. In this tale, a glamorous older woman transforms a young girl's miserable time at the dance by sharing her lipstick.

could be as lovely as Lucile. Would it be better to dream or do?

The mayor's daughter disappeared into the local drug store. Some distance away a distinguished car horn blared forth. The crowd broke out with a roar.

Gail Godwin

🖙 *In* The Finishing School, *14-year-old Justin is "enchanted" by artistic Ursula DeVane. Justin buys a bottle of the same body lotion she noticed in the woman's house, and, while rubbing it on herself, pretends to become her mentor. In "Some Side Effects of Time Travel," Gretchen performs a similar body-lotion ritual in honor of her idol, Mother Maloney.*

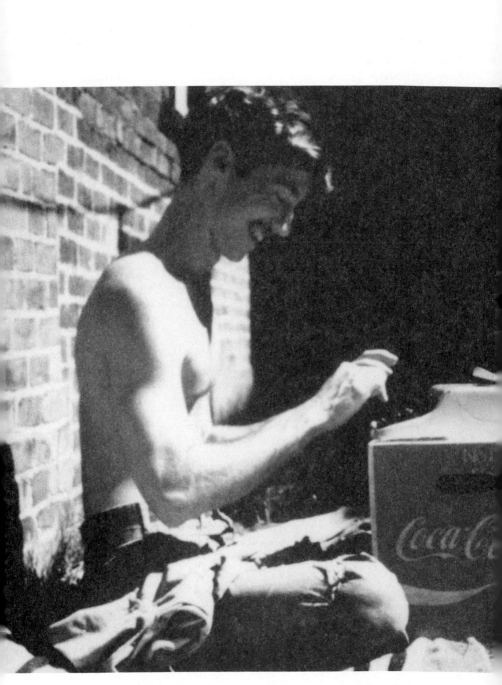

Allan Gurganus at age 18, in Navy work clothes, Boston Naval Shipyard, writing fiction

allan
gurganus

A LLAN GURGANUS MADE HIS literary debut in 1974, creating the first gay protagonist to appear in a *New Yorker* short story. The work had been submitted, without Gurganus's knowledge, by his mentor and admirer John Cheever. Fifteen years later Gurganus made an even bigger entrance with the publication of his first book, the acclaimed, best-selling novel *Oldest Living Confederate Widow Tells All*. It's a huge book, big-mouthed and big-hearted. Gloria Naylor, in her judge's report for the Book of the Month Club, wrote, according to *New York* magazine, that "she felt as deeply for Gurganus's Confederate citizens as she did for their slaves."

In "Garden Sermon" (1989), an essay about his novel's origins, Gurganus tells how, in 1968, soon after being forced into the military, he made the ironic and upsetting discovery that his ancestors had been slave owners. That realization directed Gurganus to an engrossing and ever-widening theme: the moral consequences of one person's subservience to another.

"Garden Sermon" also traces the author's voice to its beginnings. In the essay, Gurganus characterizes himself in this way: "I start as a stupidly well-brought up young man, a young whitie, of middle class privilege, of country club dances, in North Carolina. . . ." In reading the excerpt from "Just the Idea of Being in Georgia" that follows, we join with this young man—eighteen years after his birth in Rocky Mount, North Carolina, in 1947 and shortly before he will discover his own disturbing southern legacy.

Gurganus introduces his story:

I'm grateful this anthology made me face a dusty manilla folder, one stowed in closeted shame for years, one bound by rubber bands already dried to death when Lyndon Johnson led us, a binder marked, even by me, even then when so very young: "Early."

Just as our fingerprints remain constant from infancy to senility—so persists our adoration of what we each consider the most sating and ideal sentence. There from the start, our peculiar metronomic underlying prose rhythm, our cranky sense of humor, our visual gluttony, our moral preoccupations. I study this, the opening of a slightly mechanical very early short story. It seems markedly influenced by the painterly young Updike and by Flannery O'Connor, that builder of gorgeous ethical bear-traps her characters must step into being themselves gorgeous and ethical bear-traps. I see I am already preoccupied by questions of racial justice. I am interested in the mysteriously predetermined characters of obdurate children. I'm tracing the distance between dreamed Edens and actual family auto vacations. Decades later, these obsessions transmigrate across reams of paper, over changes of address and saddening hair loss; these preoccupations span a life lived despite one's better judgment: they each survive, reincarnated in my novels and stories. And in my book of novellas, *The Practical Heart*.

This fragment of an "Early" tale strikes me—a long time teacher of writing—as heartening for some reasons, hopeless for others. The narrative's attempt to create complacent trust-funded foils seems heavy-handed and very very young. But this fragment is heartening in its love of detail, its crude willingness to begin inside a dream (something I'd never do now), and mainly in its punch-drunk love of language. And yet, on the basis of this sliver alone, I might not predict a life of daily writing for this ethically certain and therefore quite satirical young man. What struck Mr. "Early" as sophisticated strikes me now as endearingly naive.

Here's a writing exercise for you: Go find your birth certificate; study your own baby fingerprints. Look, they're no bigger than punctuation! Now, ink your grizzled adult hand; press it down beside that helpless little chimp pawprint. Recognize yourself, already formed there on the baby page, helplessly and already so . . . so damn . . . you. Then weep.

Or sigh, rejoicing. Alternate the shaking of your head side to side with rueful grateful laughter. Your case has been on file since Time's efficient Hall of Records got constructed eons back: your subject matter was decided then. And the writing that you're doing now, is it being saved in a binder marked "Middle" or one marked "Late"?

Tell me I can yet progress. Don't call me A Major Novelist; let me be an inkling. Say I have, at least, a chance someday to get it right.

Curve your left palm against my right cheek and lie to me: Tell me, "Baby? It's still Early. Baby? You're still Early." ℰ

from
JUST THE IDEA OF
BEING IN GEORGIA
(1965, AGE 18)

Luther's Dream

Luther Smythe dreamed he and his family were sitting, quite naked, on a very white beach. How peaceful and ridiculous our life is here, he thought, smiling at his wife, Millie. Her eyes flirted over the green husk of coconut she seemed to be drinking from. Earlier, the children had been kicking sand at one another and wading at the edge of the azure water but they had now settled down nearby. Dennis, their son, sat smoothing sand over a second green coconut. His blonde hair sunbleached blonder shone oddly in the tropical light. Some slight distance from them, facing inland, their daughter, Cora, sat, stripped of everything but her perpetual expression, pouting even here in paradise. Her chest, so recently like her brother's, was changed, Luther saw. Her faint nipples seemed to be pouting, too. Millie saw Luther watching Cora. She dropped her coconut on the sand and crawled over to her husband on all fours, her own breasts framed, pendulous between her stiff, moving arms. Sand flew as she scrambled toward him. Luther noticed abruptly that only he was clothed, wearing the paint-splattered khakis he used for working in their little garden back in Cambridge. Millie crawled up, knelt beside him and whispered into his ear, over the sound of the surf which he'd not noticed until now, "Cora bores me, Luther. She is our daughter, certainly, but can children be bores? I think Cora's one."

Cora would likely ☞ have been denied entrance to the paradise Gurganus envisions in his 1997 novel Plays Well with Others. *As the orientation angel explains to the newest group of inductees, "You winged ones escaped your century's major peril: self-pity's flypaper."*

II

Luther woke with the conviction that they should all go to the tropics, the sooner the better. Four weeks later, at sixty miles an hour, they were returning from a compromised fulfillment of his dream, two weeks camping in Florida.

A long dent in the radiator grill gave the snoutish front of the Citroen the look of a squint or grimace. Two years earlier, the left rear door snapped open while turning a corner. It refused afterwards to shut and had since been tied closed with the cord of a broken Venetian blind. Headed due north on US 301, Luther Smythe drove the Citroen wagon he'd bought new eleven years ago with money his parents gave him when he finally got his Master's from

Obsessed with finding his old Civil War battle sites, Captain Willie Marsden loads his pregnant wife (later known as Oldest Living Confederate Widow) and eight small children ☞ into the Model T for a three-week road trip that, like Luther's trek, examines some North-South scars.

Harvard. An aluminum canoe, longer than the car, was overturned on top of it, held there by a network of twine and ropes. The car wore it like a helmet with numerous chinstraps. Millie's red bandanna, so recently her halter, had been tied to the back end of the boat and now swam straight out behind it. Provisions packed under the overturned canoe had been wrapped in a clear plastic tarpaulin. Most of this covering was unfastened after two hundred miles of wind, and it now whipped and billowed up out of the canoe, smothering, then releasing the red bandanna. The tarpaulin fanned out feet behind the car like some theatrical equivalent of water.

Inside the car was quieter. After a last Florida breakfast, all slept but Luther who sat, contentedly, hands around the wheel, feeling in control of more somehow than just the car. Autonomous, he thought; I feel distinctly autonomous. The white shirt he wore was half-buttoned and some tanned ribs showed. The khaki pants were splattered with yellow housepaint and flecks of red clay from a ceramics class he'd taken. The road came in to him through smudged tortoiseshell glasses, mended at the nosebridge with a grimy loop of adhesive tape.

Just across the state line, Luther felt a sudden pleasurable contempt for all the sleeping residents of Georgia, and then, an equally irrational pity for them. The night before, he'd explained to the children while they roasted marshmallows how, until Northern people like their father had come down to demonstrate how wrong it was, there had been public bathrooms marked "White Ladies", and others marked "Colored Women". Over their speared marshmallows, the children had eyed him suspiciously. It pleased him that they could not conceive of this sort of cruelty.

Confederate soldier Willie Marsden, newly home from the Civil War, pities his mother, injured in the burning of the family mansion—but even more, perhaps, he pities her former, vain, ☜ indulged self.

Young, white Lucy Marsden ponders uncomfortably the segregation of "Baby Africa," the shack ghetto on the outskirts of turn-of- ☜ the-century Falls, N.C.

Luther's Dream

Luther Smythe dreamed he and his family were sitting, quite naked, on a very white beach. How peaceful and ridiculous our life is here, he thought, smiling at his ~~beautiful~~ wife, Millie. Her eyes flirted over the green husk of ~~a large~~ coconut she seemed to be drinking from. Earlier, the children had been kicking sand at one another and wading at the edge of the azure water but they had now settled down nearby. Dennis, their son, sat smoothing sand over a second green coconut. His blonde hair sunbleached blonder shone oddly in the tropical light. Some slight distance from them, facing inland, their daughter, Cora, sat, stripped of everything but her perpetual expression, pouting even here in paradise. Her chest, so recently like her brother's, was changed, Luther saw. Her faint nipples seemed to be pouting, too. Millie saw Luther watching Cora. She dropped her coconut on the sand and crawled over to her husband on all fours, her own breasts framed, pendulous between her stiff, moving arms. Sand flew as she scrambled toward him. Luther noticed abruptly that only he was clothed, wearing the paint-splattered khakis he used for working in their little garden back in Cambridge.   Millie crawled up, knelt beside him and whispered into his ear, over the sound of the surf which he'd not noticed until now, "Cora bores me, Luther. She _is_ our daughter, certainly, but can children be bores? I think Cora's one."

He now scanned the landscape for what he'd always imagined as the essential meanness of Georgia, a quality so real to him he'd assumed the vegetation would reflect it by being, as he pictured the residents, all scrubby and gnarled. Maybe I've misimagined a few details, Luther conceded as he eyed suspiciously the passing farmland; the foliage _may_ be lush, but the meanness is not gone. This early on a Sunday morning, it is still stretched out somewhere, snoring.

For a moment, a delicate fear like stagefright came over him, and he wished the others were awake to help him watch for whatever it was he was expecting, but he dismissed this, finally, as ridiculous and let himself be soothed by the sound of his automobile moving himself and his sleepers straight through and out of Georgia. Having just spent seventy dollars in preventive repairs to the aging car, Luther felt the Citroen now repaying all his trust in it.

Savoring the lack of traffic, he felt exempt from all the usual daytime irritations. The children had slept, then woke and bickered inventively for an hour, and now, after breakfast, they had fallen back to sleep again. The car moved through thin strands of mist still stretched across the highway at this hour and, gazing through the dampness these left on the windshield, Luther felt refreshed, a new man ready to forget what had annoyed him on the trip down: the dashboard ashtray full of Millie's cigarette butts, missing their usual lipstick stains since vacation began, the silver casing and dangling wires of a stereo casette tape player that had been yanked, semi-professionally, out of the car in the guarded parking lot of Bonwit Teller in Boston which apologized but would not assume responsibility. Nor did he see the few remaining tape cartridges, left behind as if in judgement on the Smythe's musical taste: a Segovia one, for instance, just to the left of his sleeping wife's red polished toenails. Luther, rather, drove on, as far as the car would go with the gas depressed as fast as his blue deck shoe could press it.

Haiku had been his hobby since undergraduate days. And now slightly exceeding the Georgia speed limit as a matter of principle, the bow of his over-turned canoe forming a cozy eave, a widow's peak over the landscape, with his small, planned family,

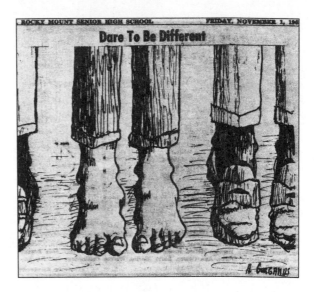

Gurganus drew this cartoon for his high school newspaper. "At 17, I was in love with how unlike others I was," he writes in his essay "Garden Sermon."

In Gurganus's story "Adult Art" (1988), ☞ a school superintendent (and former art history major) similarly harbors, beneath his quiet outer life, an erotically charged aesthetic. With haiku-like brevity, he captures the beauty of his current object of desire this way: "A vein in his neck beats like a clock, only liquid."

so recently well-fed, simplified by sleep all around him, Luther fiddled happily with words, stress, syllables, all bent on praising aspects of an almost over-ripe papaya he had enjoyed at breakfast. Occasionally, he muttered a line aloud to himself, sometimes slowly repeating it a different way. "The juice's route down chin. . .The spilled pink juice lives now in the napkin. . .briefly tinting a man's mouth. . . tinting pink briefly." Fifteen minutes passed quietly like this, one twenty fourth of Georgia.

War and Peace slipped off his wife's lap and fell face down onto the sandy floor, trapping an orange peel. Luther looked over at Millie. She stirred slightly, reached up, still asleep, and using her index finger, scratched, with delightful accuracy, the very tip of her sunburned nose. Her arm fell back to her lap. The soundness of her sleep had always seemed to him, at better moments, her attempt to compensate for his insomnia. He silently admired her, head back, brown neck taut. He looked quickly to the uneventful highway and back at Millie and back and forth.

She was as tanned now as when he met her at a party in Bermuda fifteen years ago. She had been seated, in her white dress, on a white rattan lawn chair and he'd assumed she was French until, finally introduced, she lifted her hand to him and spoke forth in the very voice of Radcliffe College, a glib, opinionated girl, interested, she said that night, in "everything and nothing". Over the miles, her skirt had inched its way up her brown thighs, slightly glossed, as if polished. One of her sandaled feet was twisted at a poignant angle, resting on its side, and her opened legs, crammed voluptuously into the space under the dashboard, pleased him to look down at.

Captain Marsden also indulges in pleasurable, proprietary visions of his young bride, picturing her at home in bed every half hour. He suggests that they synchronize their day so that he can accurately imagine her at certain moments touching herself.

Allan Gurganus

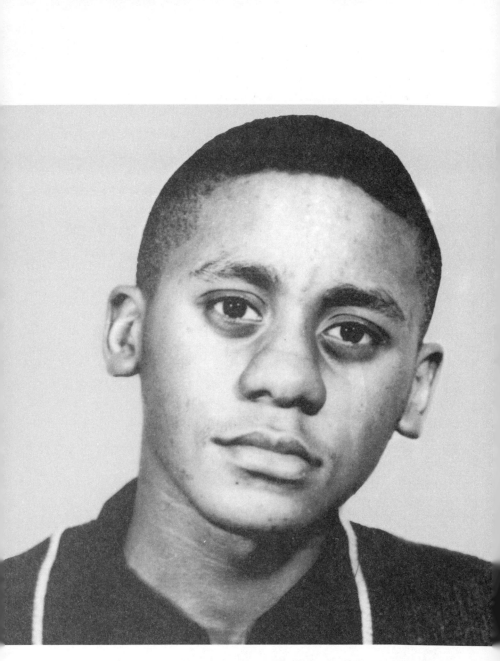

Charles Johnson took this self-portrait to fulfill a high school photography assignment

charles johnson

CHARLES JOHNSON GAINED WIDE recognition when he won the 1990 National Book Award for his novel *Middle Passage*. Johnson's fourth book of fiction, *Middle Passage* is about a newly freed bondman, who, in order to escape some debts and a romantic commitment, stows aboard an Africa-bound slave ship, on which he undergoes a voyage of self-discovery. The novel is suffused with philosophy (the subject of the author's graduate studies), politics (an interest since high school), and religion (Johnson describes himself as an "on-again-off-again Buddhist")—all the while spinning its sea story. And in this multifaceted way it explores a key Johnson theme: the Self's journeys across racial, class, cultural, and other boundaries—a theme with which the author was already experimenting in his late teens. Of the three pieces of prose that follow, the first two were composed for a high school creative writing class and appeared in a school publication; the third is a letter to the editor of his college newspaper.

"I never saw myself as a writer," says Johnson of his youth. In high school, writing was a sideline while he devoted himself to his true passion, cartooning. He drew a comic strip, "Wonder Wildkit," coproduced bimonthly with a classmate, and contributed illustrations to the high school paper.

Born in Evanston, Illinois, in 1948, Johnson, an only child, describes himself as having been a "serious kid . . . very introspective" and pensive about "the world around me. Why it was the way it was. I don't think it's easy to be a black kid growing up in the fifties and be frivolous."

He credits his mother with fueling his intellectual and artistic curiosity (she often brought home discarded books from the Northwestern University sorority where she worked). His father, a city employee, exerted a more businesslike influence and once signed Johnson up for a surprise summer job: "Doing what?" asked Johnson, just home from college for a summer break. "You're a garbage man," his father announced.

"He taught me how to work," says the author and 1998 recipient of the illustrious MacArthur "Genius" Award. ✑

MAN BENEATH RAGS
(1965, AGE 17)

Evening was growing colder as the white-collar workers scurried home to warm fires and after-dinner pipes. A large pair of eyes, half closed by cataracts, watched them with uncomprehending envy. Calloused hands rubbed vigorously together to fight the chilling night air, as a bent back leaned against a locked doorway. A doorway that is always locked.

Another human shuck in tattered cloth joined him on his doorstep throne. Exchanging names was unnecessary. Two pair of eyes, tired and bored, watched humanity passing. Exhausted minds recalled better days, happier moments, dead ambitions. Thick tongues licked long, drooping lips as a half-empty flask sprang from the remains of a once-proud jacket, and into a hand that welcomed the friendship which the decanter offered. The bottle was passed without a word. They were silent strangers, and in some way also brothers, united in defeat and misery.

A dark figure with a dangling nightstick rounded the corner, and trod silently towards them. Auto-

Rutherford Calhoun, the wayward freedman in Middle Passage, *recognizes his kinship with the* Allmuseri *slaves below deck and other fellow sufferers aboard the* Republic. ☞

matically they rose and separated, leaving behind a
thousand silent companions. They didn't run. They
were still men.

50 CARDS 50
(1966, AGE 17)

Richard stared in awe at the glistening Christmas
tree before him. Little silver angels and stars gleamed
from each branch as the huge pine illuminated the
entire room. There were no presents under the tree,
but Richard was, nevertheless, the happiest boy in
Harlem.

As he sat arranging a nativity scene, the apartment doorbell chimed, and his mother admitted a
portly mulatto woman bearing ribboned packages.
Richard ignored them; like most eight-year-old boys,
his thoughts were on Santa Claus, the rotund deity
who would deliver gifts to children throughout the

**Johnson drew this accompanying illustration
for his high school paper.**

"Why can't I imagine
a white Santa Claus?"
asks the adult author.
In this story, Johnson
laments the "racial
polarization" that has
suddenly been imposed
on a boy who "wasn't
thinking about race."

world. Richard was wondering how Santa would enter their apartment since it lacked a chimney. They certainly couldn't leave the door open—not in *their* neighborhood.

The cheerful "goodbye" and "Merry Christmas" of the mulatto woman aroused Richard from his fantasies. He noticed a tempting package on the sofa across the room. His mother must have bought it from the woman who had just left. After reassuring himself that his mother had returned to her kitchen chores, Richard stole across the room, and gave vent to childish curiosity by unwrapping the box. His nervous fingers lifted the lid and a chocolate Santa Claus grinned foolishly at him, as his sleigh drew him across the narrow width of cardboard. There were fifty such cards in the box, and Richard stared dumbly at them for long minutes.

These were not the jolly men with rosy cheeks and button noses that he had seen on street corners, jangling bells and seeking charity. They were not like the red-suited Santas he had seen inside the shiny pages of the magazines his mother brought home. For some reason, the ebony Santa was meant for him, alone. For some peculiar reason which he could not grasp, he was not supposed to visualize a Santa Claus with bright cheeks and a merry, red nose. Richard suddenly realized that the room was strangely dark, and he no longer cared how Santa entered their apartment.

Even though he thought his son's ambition to become a
cartoonist impractical, Johnson's father funded two years of
correspondence art classes. Johnson went on to publish
more than a thousand drawings, including these samples of
a high school comic strip (opposite), as well as the
King drawings on page 114.

INDIVIDUALITY, NOT COLLECTIVITY, IS VEHICLE FOR ATTAINING EQUALITY

(1968, AGE 20)

To the Daily Egyptian:

Much ado about race is made with justification these days, and virtually everyone agrees that the desirable end of all civil rights endeavors should be universal equality. The means for attaining this goal is undoubtedly where our conflict arises. Sprouting

Johnson's 1998 novel *Dreamer* takes a fresh look at Martin Luther King and tries to answer the question of how one becomes a saint. He published this editorial cartoon in his college newspaper in 1968.

up everywhere are a myriad of self-appointed groups, black and white, who assume their union of forces will somehow alleviate the current race crisis.

If equality and eventual brotherhood are the goals in sight, the vehicle for attaining this goal must lie within the individual, not in collective forces. The individual must undergo the grueling chore of recognizing himself as a unique entity and define his own goals, strengths and weaknesses.

Having done so, he will be in a position to appreciate and respect others who have done the same, and perhaps be eager to help those who still struggle with their existence.

The progress of race relations must take place in the enlightenment of the individuals that compose our society, not in the groups who sacrifice the individual for a collective intelligence.

In Being and Race: Black Writing since 1970, *his 1988 book of literary criticism and philosophy, Johnson takes issue with certain racially based arts movements for deemphasizing the individual.*

Charles Johnson

Stephen King at age 9, with Queenie

stephen king

K IDS ARE BENT," WRITES Stephen King in *Danse Macabre*
(1981), his survey of contemporary horror. They still have the imagination to "think around corners." This faculty fades, he adds, with
the coming of adulthood — except perhaps in fantasy-horror writers, such as
King, whose job "is to make you, for a little while, a child again."

Readers often presume a deep-rooted deviance on the part of the fantasy-
horror practitioner, inspiring such questions, King writes, as, "Was your
mother scared by a two-headed dog while you were *in utero?*" As a four-year-
old, King might have seen a playmate killed by a train (King's mother told
him years later that he had come home in shock). Upon hearing King
recount this story at a mystery writers' convention, one psychiatrist-novelist
asserted that King had been writing about the childhood event ever since.

King dismisses the train incident as a motive for his career. He does,
however, point to this crystallizing moment: his discovery, at about age
twelve, of a cache of fantasy-horror paperbacks in his aunt's attic. These
works by H. P. Lovecraft and others were left behind by King's father, who
abandoned the family when King was two years old. The father had tried his
hand at horror stories but never published any and lacked, according to
King's mother, a "stick-to-it . . . nature."

King himself possesses this nature in abundance. He has published
(under both his own name and the pen name Richard Bachman) more
than thirty books of fiction, including the novels *Carrie* (1974), *The Shining*
(1977), *The Stand* (1978), *Misery* (1987), and *Bag of Bones* (1998).

Born in Portland, Maine, in 1947, King has lived in the state most of his life. A quiet child, he wrote the following story at age nine for his Aunt Gert, described in a recent letter to his agent as "my first patron. She was amused by my story-writing hobby and used to pay me a quarter a story. Naturally I inundated her!"

"By the way," the letter adds, "one thing about the enclosed should make you feel that entropy doesn't *always* apply; you'll note that at least my spelling has gotten better."

Given that King and others have made the connection between fairy tales and horror stories, it seems fitting that the following early King effort is indeed in a Grimm mode. Like his hero, "Jhonathan . . . the cobblers son," King has gone on to seek out his share of evils and been rewarded with great riches. ✑

JHONATHAN AND THE WITCHS

(CIRCA 1956, AGE 9)

Once upon a time there was a boy named Jhonathan. He was smart, handsome, and very brave. But Jhonathan was a cobblers son.

One day his father said, "Jhonathan, you must go and seek your fortune. You are old enough."

Jhonathan, being a smart boy knew he better ask the King for work.

So, he set out.

On the way, he met a rabbit who was a fariy in disguise. The scared thing was being pursued by hunters and jumped into Jhonathans arms. When the hunters came up Jhonathan pointed excitedly and shouted, "That way, that way!"

After the hunters had gone, the rabbit turned into

King, who also grew 🖝 *up in a household of modest means, is still partial to child protagonists, especially underdogs, like Carrie and like the kids who make up the Losers' Club in* It.

a fairy and said, "You have helped me. I will give you three wishes. What are they?"

But Jhonathan could not think of anything, so the fairy agreed to give them to him when he needed them.

So, Jhonathan kept walking until he made the kingdom without incedent.

So he went to the king and asked for work.

But, as luck would have it, the king was in a very bad mood that day. So he vented his mood on Jhonathan.

"Yes, there is something you can do. On yonder Mountain there are three witches. If you can kill them, I will give you 5,000 crowns. If you cannot do it I will have your head! You have 20 days." With this he dismissed Jhonathan.

Now what am I to do? thought Jhonathan. Well I shall try.

Then he remembered the three wishes granted him and set out for the mountain.

In the author's short story "Word Processor of the Gods" (1983), an unappreciated husband finds he can control reality with his newfangled computer. The story is a high-tech twist on the traditional wish tale.

*   *   *   *

Now Jhonathan was at the mountain and was just going to wish for a knife to kill the witch, when he heard a voice in his ear, "The first witch cannot be peirced.

The second witch cannot be perced or smothered.

The third cannot be perced, smothered and is invisable.

With this knolege Jhonathen looked about and saw noone. Then he remembered the fairy, and smiled.

He then went in search of the first witch.

At last he found her. She was in a cave near the foot of the mountain, and was a mean looking hag.

He remembered the fairy words, and before the

JHONATHAN AND the Withs
By Stephen King

Once upon a time there was a boy named Jhonathan.
He was smart, handsome, and very brave. But, Jhonathan was a cobblers son.

One day his father said, "Jhonathan, you must go and seek your fourtune. You are old enough."

Jhonathan, being a smart boy knew he better ask the King for work.

So, he set out.

On the way, he met a Rabbit who was a fairy in disguise. The scared thing was being pursued by hunters and jumped into Jhonathans arms. When the hunters came up Jhonathan pointed excitedly and shouted, "That way, that way!"

After the hunters had gone, the Rabbit turned into a fairy and said, "You have helped me. I will give you three wishes. What are they?"

But Jhonathan could not think of anything, so the fairy agreed to give them to him when he needed them.

So, Jhonathan kept walking untill he made the kingdom withatt incedent.

So he went to the King and asked for work.

But, as luck would have it, the King was in a very bad mood that day. So he vented his mood on Jhonathan.

witch could do anything but give him an ugly look, he wished she should be smothered. And Lo! It was done.

Now he went higher in search of the second witch. There was a second cave higher up. There he found the second witch. He was about to wish her smothered when he remembered she could not be smothered. And then before the witch could do anything but give him an ugly look, he had wished her crushed. And Lo! It was done.

Now he had onley to kill the third witch and he would have the 5,000 crowns. But on the way up, he was plauged with thoughts of how?

Then he hit upon a wonderful plan.

Then, he saw the last cave. He waited outsid the entrance until he heard the witches footsteps. He then picked up a couple of big rocks and wished.

He then wished the witch a normal woman and Lo! She became visable and then Jhonathen struck her dead with the rocks he had.

Jhonathan collected his 5,000 crowns and he and his father lived happily ever after.

☜ Carrie, the title character in King's first published novel, similarly has merely to wish for something to happen and it does, through telekinesis. In that fairy tale gone awry, however, Carrie also plays one of several witchlike parts.

Stephen King

Maxine Hong, age 16, as editor of her high school newspaper

maxine hong kingston

WHEN I FIRST BEGAN to write," says Maxine Hong Kingston, "I thought of writing as an act of cowardice," a chance to vent feelings without confrontation. And so, not surprisingly, her journal entry about the night of the disastrous dance, written when she was fourteen, reads like a private complaint. By the time she became editor of her high school newspaper, however, she had worked up enough courage to take some of her concerns public. Today her mature work is respected for, among other things, its conviction and bravery.

She established herself as a writer in 1976 with her memoir *The Woman Warrior*. In it she recalls a Chinese-American girlhood haunted by racism, sexism, the past, and her uncertainty about the boundaries between fact and myth. After a companion work of creative nonfiction, *China Men* (1980), she published her first novel, *Tripmaster Monkey*, in 1989. Like the younger self Maxine Hong Kingston describes in *The Woman Warrior*, protagonist Wittman Ah Sing is a rebel, a social critic sustained by a vision of justice, willing and able to deliver a blazing editorial when necessary.

Born in Stockton, California, in 1940, Maxine Hong was shy as a small child. In middle childhood, a "mysterious illness" kept her bedridden for more than a year, and she went through a phase, which she describes humorously in *The Woman Warrior*, when she worried about her habit of conversing with imaginary beings. By the book's end, however, she has come into her own, finding in high school validation for her future career.

"I may be ugly and clumsy," she tells her parents, trying to assert herself during a teenage outburst, "but. . . . I'm so smart, if they say write ten pages, I can write fifteen."

Just days after Maxine Hong Kingston contributed the following samples of her juvenilia, the rest of her childhood writings—as well as her manuscript in progress and her entire home—were consumed in the October 1991 fires that ravaged the Oakland Hills. ℰ

JOURNAL ENTRY, JULY 7
(1955, AGE 14)

My Louisville Slugger bats arrived. They're not *really* bats. They're a pen and pencil set with holders like bats. Only cost me $.50 (cents). Writes nice, doesn't it? Ted William's and Ralph Kiner's autographs are on them.

This is my new notebook—since the other is filled.

I hope this helps rush in the spirit of summer.

There are 66 days of vacation left.

I bought a thick note-book about three times the size of this. I'm going to write stories in it. (I don't like to type them.

This note-book is supposed to have a picture of the Cisco Kid on it; a picture of Jane Wyman on the other.

JOURNAL ENTRY, JULY 15

(1955, AGE 14)

Went to club, Theta Pi, dance—Rhythm & Blues. Had miserable time—First dance of mine. Of course we had to work because we were giving the dance—People just leave their manners at home when they come to dances it seems. They come & show off—and act up—even people that I *used* to think were at least O.K.—People, trying to sneak in for free—People rude, noisy, boastrous, gossipy—.

Its pitiful—after we worked *so* putting up decorations and everything in the ladies room & all—they tore them down—laughed—Its mean—absolutely so! Priscilla heard someone make remarks about my pigtails—If a person can't say a thing to another's face—they're cowards to say them behind their backs. No, I don't expect people to be perfect but at least they could try. At least we took in $9.08—about $5 profit.—Hope we never give another dance again—never, never, never, never!!!!!!!

Corrinne had her tonsils out yesterday. I gave her lots of presents—paper dolls, put together animals—about nine presents in all—for her to open on different days but she is impatient & opened them all at once.

Today I went to the movies with Priscilla & Bonnie at the Esquire. We had to wait in line in the lobby for seats—there were so many people! We saw Tex Barker in "Bitter Ridge"—a western & Donald O'Conner in "Frances Joins the Navy." Both good and entertaining.

M.H.

Wittman Ah Sing, the poet protagonist of Tripmaster Monkey, *is often confronted with behavior he finds ☜ offensive. "Normal humanity," he remarks early in the book, "mean and wrong."*

☜ Corrinne is the author's sister.

July '74 1—

July 15 1955
Went to club, Theta Pi, dance—
Rhythm & Blues. Had miserable
time. 1st dance of
mine. Of course we
had to work because we were
giving the dance. People
just leave their manners
at home when they come
to dances it seems. They
come & show off
and act up even
people that I used to
think were at least
O.K. People, trying
to sneak in for free.
People crude, noisy,
brashness, pushing.

COLLECTIONS
(1956, AGE 15–16)

a. stuffed animals
b. art prints
c. pattern ads
d. articles on authors
e. [or *l*] green clothing
m. perfumes, esp. French

Friends and relatives through the years have urged Wittman Ah Sing (in Tripmaster Monkey) *not to wear green, because, he is finally told, "'We look yellow in that color.' It had to do with racial skin. And, of course, from that time on, he knew what color he had to wear — green. . . ."*

IN MY OPINION
(1957, AGE 16)

Women can out-think, out-talk and out-smart men, and those are proved facts.

The author regularly wrote this column for her high school newspaper.

Didn't Joan of Arc, Maid of Orleans, send the British forces flying before her inspired army until Charles was crowned king at Rheims? Wasn't it Elizabeth Cady Stanton's, Lucretia Mott's and Susan B. Anthony's burning orations for women's suffrage, which fired the forges of male-partisaned government to cast the die for a nineteenth amendment to the Constitution? And wasn't it Cleopatra who led Caesar to war, Ptolemy to oblivion, and Anthony to a lifetime of servitude?

Then why, pray tell, are men endowed with certain inalienable rights which we women are denied? Why are they bestowed with the privilege of having a second lunch period for luncheon meetings, while

In My Opinion
by Maxine Hong

Women can out-think, out-talk and out-smart men, and those are proved facts.

Didn't Joan of Arc, Maid of Orleans, send the British forces flying before her inspired army until Charles was crowned king at Rheims? Wasn't it Elizabeth Cady Stanton's, Lucretia Mott's, and Susan B. Anthony's burning orations for women's suffrage, which fired the forges of male-partisaned government to cast the die for a n i n e teenth amendment to the C o n s t i tution? And wasn't it Cleopatra who led Caesar to war, Ptolemy to oblivion, and Anthony to a lifetime of servitude?

Maxine Hong

Then why, pray tell, are men endowed with certain inalienable rights which we women are denied? Why are they bestowed with the privilege of having a second lunch period for luncheon meetings, while we girls slave on in class? Why can they have a Key Club for "outstanding" boys, while we have nothing?

There are girls with leadership qualities and a creditable amount of brains, too, you know. We deserve something. After all, girls can do anything boys can — and better, too.

* * *

I've got it figured out at last why there was such an outbreak of resorting to fisticuffs near the fifty wing and in the . . . er . . . establishments (shall we say?) across the street just before Christmas vacation. It was Peterson Hall! Why, they have a ball up there at Christmas time. There's gifts from everybody — the San Joaquin County Farm Bureau, Salvation Army, Junior Red Cross, Civitan Club, First Christian Church, North Stockton Kiwanis, Manteca Cub Scout Pack 35, Rho Mu Sorority, and the 521st Engineer Company. Those comic books had me disillusioned. Crime does too pay.

* * *

Four Negro churches were dynamited recently in Alabama. A Virginia newspaper asked the Supreme Court to reverse its integration decision since there was such an "amount of evidence before it of the enormous opposition in the South."

Why, Thomas Jefferson must have turned over in his grave. As a Virginian, he, too, had written about men's rights; but he said that "all men are created equal." A Negro's a man; so's a Caucasian, and a Mongolian, too. That makes us all equal. Who can deny that "quantities equal to the same quantity are equal?" It's proof—geometric proof—and no Southern rebel can tell me different.

we girls slave on in class? Why can they have a Key Club for "outstanding" boys, while we have nothing?

There are girls with leadership qualities and a creditable amount of brains, too, you know. We deserve something. After all, girls can do anything boys can—and better, too. [. . .]

* * * *

Four Negro churches were dynamited recently in Alabama. A Virginia newspaper asked the Supreme Court to reverse its integration decision since there was such an "amount of evidence before it of the enormous opposition in the South."

Why, Thomas Jefferson must have turned over in his grave. As a Virginian, he, too, had written about men's rights; but he said that "all men are created equal." A Negro's a man; so's a Caucasian, and a Mongolian, too. That makes us all equal. Who can deny that "quantities equal to the same quantity are equal?" It's proof—geometric proof—and no Southern rebel can tell me different.

> 🖎 *The double standard applied to girls seems especially rigid among the older, Chinese-born men that Maxine Hong Kingston describes in* The Woman Warrior. *In one scene, her great-uncle makes his preference for grandsons quite clear. Pointing to the six girls consuming food at the dinner table, he calls each of them a maggot.*

"I minded that the emigrant villagers shook their heads at my sister and me. 'One girl—and another girl,' they said," writes Maxine Hong Kingston in The Woman Warrior. *"The good part about my brothers being born was that people stopped saying, 'All girls'. . . ."* (Norman Hong is the author's brother.)

I just won two honor award ribbons for my printing and silk screening at the San Joaquin County California Industrial Education Association Festival. They were both won under Norman's name however. (Mr. Britt's idea) because girls just don't enter industrial art shop festivals.

MH

Maxine Hong's winning silk-screen print. "The elf's name is Wit (like my character Wittman)," says the author.

Now for the unhappier part of life—and boy(!) it's really tear-jerking. My grades are hitting bottom—not rock bottom either—slimy, pulling, quick-sandy bottom. Miss Trachiotis is giving objective instead of essay tests now and I hate those!!

Doug Kim is trying to get MY column for himself come next year! We had a good old argument about it the other day. I told him the feature page was MY page and he wasn't going to write MY column as long as I was here and as long as I'M editor of MY feature page. He told me he *was* as long as it was HIS newspaper and HE was the editor-in-chief. That's what he thinks—CAUSE NOBODY IS GOING TO WRITE "IN MY OPINION" AS LONG AS I AM A MEMBER OF EDISON SENIOR HIGH SCHOOL. Then we started arguing about writing editorials. He told me he was going to write *all* of the editorials!! I told him he wasn't as long as editorials were on the second page. We—or I, at least—decided if he had an idea, he'd write it. If I had an idea, I'd write! Professional rivalry is bringing rivals to a state of dueling now.

Then there's the matter of E[—] E[—] R[—]. She got caught smoking! She's been expelled!!! At first it was just probation—but now she's expelled!! She can't receive a single solitary award at the assembly —and she's earned a lot from her music—believe me!! I don't care what Mrs. Rovetta might say—but to me smoking is not immoral. There's nothing wrong with it. Why, even Father smokes! This punishment was too severe! I don't know why she's taking it out so hard on E[—] E[—].

Maxine Hong Kingston

Ursula Kroeber in 1935

ursula k. le guin

I WENT UP TO THE trunk in the attic, a yellow footlocker actually, and explored," reports Ursula K. Le Guin in a letter to *First Words*. Unfortunately, she could not find her story, written around age nine and already indicating her attraction to fantasy, about a man tormented by evil elves. ("People think he is mad, but the evil elves finally slither in through the keyhole, and get him.") Nor could she locate her first science-fiction effort from about two years later ("It involved time travel and the origin of life on Earth, and was very breezy in style"), which brought the author her first rejection slip.

She did find two poems, however, written during her first semester at college. Readers will recognize the author's self-described romantic streak, which in her mature work she blends with complex insights into social issues in such well-known novels as *The Left Hand of Darkness* (1969), *The Dispossessed: An Ambiguous Utopia* (1974), and her Earthsea series. Although much of Le Guin's adult writing is labeled science fiction, she "has purposely avoided most technical details," remarks one literary critic, "in order to concentrate on human problems and relationships."

Marriage, which the author once described as the "central, constant theme" of her work, forms the heart of her teenage poem "Song." Freedom from social roles and other such limits, another recurring Le Guin theme, predominates in her poem "December 31, 1947."

Born in Berkeley, California, in 1929, Ursula Kroeber as a child read myths and fairy tales (and "everything I could get my hands on, which was limitless") and inherited her anthropologist father's taste for fantasy literature.

Her earliest creative writing efforts were poems, which she began to commit to paper at age five, she says, once her brother Ted, "who was ashamed to discover that he had an illiterate sister," had taught her to write. While still age four, however, the young author had to dictate the first of the following poems to its subject: her mother, Theodora Kracaw Kroeber. ☙

TO KRAKIE
(1934, AGE 4)

Bears like honey,
I do too.
I like you, honey,
I sure do.

SONG
(1947, AGE 17)

No swallow follows summer
So far as I would thee:
O love, my heart goes to thee
Like a river to the sea.

All my soul is turned to dust
Or to salt sea foam:
Return, return, return to me,
My love, my heart, my home!

DECEMBER 31ST, 1947

(1947, AGE 18)

In this year nineteen-forty-seven
I have built myself to heaven
And as well
Have slung myself to hell.
In the year born tomorrow
I want no loss of sorrow,
Joy, love, madness, hate, desire, right, and evil:
God only keep me from the level,
The blind, the bland, the kingdom of the Devil!

In The Dispossessed: An Ambiguous Utopia, *the planet Urras—a world of extremes—is endorsed by the ambassador from Terra. "I know it's full of evils," she concedes, "full of human injustice, greed, folly, waste. But it is also full of good, of beauty, vitality, achievement. It is what a world should be! It is alive . . ." (whereas her own people back home have been forced, for survival's sake, into "absolute regimentation").*

Ursula K. Le Guin

Madeleine L'Engle, age 12, at Chamonix with skis and stuffed animals

madeleine l'engle

I AM STILL EVERY AGE that I have been," Madeleine L'Engle writes in her 1972 memoir *A Circle of Quiet*. "Because I was once a child, I am always a child. Because I was once a searching adolescent, given to moods and ecstasies, these are still part of me, and always will be."

Born in 1918 in New York City to a pianist and a foreign correspondent, Madeleine L'Engle grew up with an "overshy" nature. Her shyness was perhaps exacerbated by a demoralizing stint at a New York private school where she was made to feel clumsy and stupid. Creative writing became an early emotional outlet. In *A Circle of Quiet*, she describes some of the resulting juvenilia: a "sequel to the *Odyssey*, with Telemachus as the hero," and a now-lost novel about triplets who combine their various skills (academic, athletic, and social) and try to pass themselves off as one very accomplished and well-rounded person.

The search for wholeness appears not only in the story, "Six Good People," that follows, but also in her most famous work, the Newbery Medal–winning classic *A Wrinkle in Time* (1962), about three special children and their cosmic battle against insidious conformity.

The author of more than thirty books, including *The Irrational Season* (autobiography, 1977) and the novels *A Swiftly Tilting Planet* (1978), *A Severed Wasp* (1982), and *A Live Coal in the Sea* (1996), L'Engle explores the spiritual quest of the individual and the salvation of love. An openness and warmth characterize her writings for adults as well as youngsters. ☞

A BOY'S DREAM

(1929, AGE 11)

L'Engle's fanciful
imagination once
prompted a high school
chemistry incident, con-
fessed in her 1983 Library
of Congress address: "One
day while I was happily
pretending to myself that
I was Madame Curie,
I blew up the lab."

At night I go to bed and dream
I travel to strange lands afar;
Last night I visited a land,
The country where the Romans are.

I talked to a Roman Poet,
The whole world knows of his fame.
I start to read some of his poems,
They tell me Virgil is his name.

I run into Julius Cæsar,
(In the middle of the night)
And Mark Antony and others,
Dressed in armour gleaming bright.

I didn't tell my dream to Father,
For I knew that he would laugh,
The only one that listened to me
Was a new-born baby calf.

SPACE

(1932, AGE 14)

My blood runs cold when I think about the sky—
Think that it never ends—
Think that it just keeps on being sky,
And stars,
And space.
But if it did have an end—
What would be beyond that?

ETERNITY

(1932, AGE 14)

I wake up in the middle of the night
And hear the steady ticking of the clock.
Two, five, ten, seconds go by,
Never to come again.
Fifty seconds, a minute is gone . . .
More minutes come and go . . .
But minutes will keep coming throughout eternity;
Why should I worry because they go so fast?

In her memoir A Circle of Quiet, *L'Engle fondly discusses a Greek word for time,* kairos, *which, unlike* chronos, *is not measurable. "Kairos can sometimes enter, penetrate, break through* chronos: *the child at play, the painter at his easel, Serkin playing the* Appassionata, *are in* kairos."

Madeleine L'Engle at age 14, with Sputstzi

L'Engle combines the
elements of space, time, and
whimsy in tessering, the
method of timespace travel
favored by the characters of
A Wrinkle in Time. Boy
genius Charles Wallace
tries to explain the concept
to his older sister, Meg:
"The fifth dimension's a
tesseract. You add that to
the other four dimensions
and you can travel through
space without having to go
the long way around."

WHIMSEY

(1932, AGE 14)

I'd like
To fly
Up to the
Moon,
To sit on a
Moonbeam,
And slide back to
Earth.

SIX GOOD PEOPLE

(1933, AGE 15)

They had never seen each other, or even heard of
each other, yet they were from the same city, and
were destined to enter heaven on the same day and
hour. Now they were standing together, waiting for
the pearly gates to open unto them.

Mrs. Lancaster was a fine old lady with white hair
carefully dressed and beautiful clothes. Her eyes
were bright and piercing, her nose aristocratic. Her
mouth was stern and humorous and imperious.

Michael Carstairs had been on the earth only six
years. His tan hair was ruffled all over his head,
and his large wistful eyes were gazing wonderingly
around him. Occasionally he would glance down
at his thin little leg encased in a heavy brace, and a
great hope would spring into his face.

Mrs. Amanda Griggs waited shyly, twisting her gnarled hands through her black and white checked apron, or pushing back a wisp of iron-gray hair. Her wrinkled face was full of confident expectancy, and her old eyes shone with childlike faith.

Young David Mallinson stood dreamily, occasionally running his long slender hands with the spatulate fingertips through his wild brown hair, or playing a fragment of a great composition as though he sensed shining ivory keys under them.

Grenfell Dredge sketched rapidly on a small pad with quiet precision, moving his fingers over his neat mustache, his scholar's mind succeeding in absolute concentration.

Little Nan [. . .] held an old rag doll in her arm and sang to it softly, thinking with all her energetic young brain. She watched the others, and after a while went and stood by Michael, but said nothing.

And so these six good people were admitted together into heaven. The great pearly gates drew apart in a burst of joyful music, and they stepped in, the proud Mrs. Lancaster leading.

She found herself in a great ball room hung with magnificent crystal chandeliers. The music was coming from an orchestra at the far end. She stopped in front of a mirror, and saw herself young again, arrayed in the gorgeous silks and satins of her youth, her young head poised proudly, her dainty feet tapping the floor in time with the music. In a moment she was waltzing away on the arms of a young gallant. After a time there was a stir of excitement. Murmurs of "the great LaFayette!" went around. And suddenly she saw him standing before her, asking her to dance. It was the greatest honor any young girl could have. Her eyes shone as she graciously gave him her arm. "Oh, heaven!" she murmured to herself.

Due to a childhood illness,
L'Engle's legs were ☞
of uneven length, making
her an outcast in school
gym class, she writes in
A Circle of Quiet.
"I remember quite clearly
coming home in the
afternoon . . . and think-
ing, calmly and bitterly,
'I am the cripple, the
unpopular girl,' . . . and
writing a story for myself
where the heroine was the
kind of girl I would have
liked to be."

Closely following Mrs. Lancaster through the gates was young Michael Carstairs. As he entered another boy came up to him, grinned pleasantly and said "Hullo! You're the new one, aren't you? We've been expectin' you. You're just in time for the race. Come on. You're going to run, of course, aren't you? We all do." Michael looked down at his leg. It was sturdy and strong. Eagerly he followed the other boy, and in a few moments he was running down a long level course, easily keeping up with the rest. In a while he found only two boys ahead of him, the freckled lad who had met him, and a long thin one with red hair. He breathed hard and drew level with the thin boy—then with the freckled one—then he was in the lead—and had broken the tape. Great cheers were shouted, and the freckled one and several others bore him off on their shoulders. He sat upright, looking as though it didn't matter. "This is heaven," he thought.

Amanda Griggs edged humbly in, and suddenly she found herself in a great city with golden streets and voices singing in beauty. She looked at herself, and she was clad in a long white robe, and great wings were folded behind her. She raised her hand, no longer gnarled, and felt tentatively above her head. Yes, there was the halo. A great joy ran through her, and though she had never seen a harp before, she sat down before one and with the air of one greatly practised drew her fingers across the strings, and sweet music came forth. "Heaven at last!" she sighed.

David Mallinson followed the quavering Mrs. Griggs. As he stepped through the gates a great clapping arose, and he found himself in a great auditorium facing a vast audience, and bowing, once, twice, thrice. Then, slowly he raised his baton, and the music came softly from the orchestra, rising, rising, into magnificent beauty. The audience sat spellbound; no one moved. David was inspired with tremendous genius, and the music was so wonderful that it filled him with awe. "It is heavenly," he thought.

Grenfell Dredge put his pad into his pocket, followed the others, and stepped through the gates into a great observatory. A magnificent telescope occupied most of the space, and as he walked over to it he thrilled with indescribable awe—for this was the telescope that he had always dreamed of, the one that would show him far more than man had as yet been allowed to see. As he put his eye to it he murmured, "Ah heaven. Perfect knowledge!"

Nan entered last, into a most beautiful garden full of thousands of flowers, or were they flowers? Why no, of course not, they were fairies. A beautiful one fluttered up to her and in a voice that sounded like the tones one would imagine blue Canterbury bells would make swinging in the breeze told Nan that the fairy queen desired her presence. Nan eagerly followed her to a flower of perfect whiteness on a long slender green stalk. The fairy queen sat regally in its cup, dressed in a gown of rose petals. "Oh, beautiful heaven!" whispered Nan.

And so, these six good people together entered the gates of heaven.

The bond between faith and music, and the similar solace that they provide, is central to A Severed Wasp. *In describing a child's piano playing, L'Engle writes: "The gentle melody was an affirmation. Was prayer."*

Madeleine L'Engle

Jill McCorkle at age 7

jill mccorkle

I N 1984 JILL McCORKLE made a double debut with the publication of two well-received novels, *The Cheer Leader* and *July 7th*, when she was just twenty-five years old, and she has since written four more plus two collections of short stories, *Crash Diet* (1992) and *Final Vinyl Days* (1998). Her fiction explores the complexities of marriage, divorce and remarriage, daughterly bonds and aggravations, furniture refinishing, therapy, therapeutic shopping, cats, family lore, and family skeletons. A North Carolina native, born in Lumberton in 1958, McCorkle lovingly portrays the shifting scene of her home state and the New South. Her canvas is the daily life she has observed there, and her medium is storytelling that gently enfolds both the comic and melancholy.

"I wrote my first story, 'The Night Santa Failed to Come,' when I was in the second grade," she recalls.

> From then on, writing was a favorite activity, particularly if I could peddle the finished product to my parents. My profit lasted only as long as it took me to mount my bicycle and ride to what we called "the little store" and then disappeared in a little brown paper sack of Mary Janes and Bazooka gum.
>
> The summer after second grade my father brought home a huge wooden crate; it had originally housed a knitting machine delivered to a local textile mill. It was *supposed* to be a storage shed, but he had no sooner cut and hinged a door before I moved

in: pallet, tea set, dress-up clothes, my own fishing gear (another favorite activity), bricks for a faux fireplace, and bedding for my cat. He gave in. His tools remained crammed in a small storage room. My mother sewed curtains for the *new* playhouse. This became my writing place, and over the next four years much of my time was spent there. The house was sometimes opened to others as sort of a neighborhood playhouse (Rumpelstiltskin was a popular production). But for the most part it remained a private place for me and one of my biggest sources of inspiration: a huge black and white tom cat named Shon-Ton (the result of my misunderstanding the pronunciation of a French cat's name on a television program). People didn't "fix" their cats in those days and so Shon-Ton was usually sporting a few minor head wounds. The recuperating cat proved to be a wonderful audience for a long time.

My motivation when writing these stories was to get a laugh or a tear. I *had* to have a response. "The Twins" was written on this wonderful cool and rainy afternoon when I was experiencing what I'd now call an enjoyable cleansing kind of melancholia, but then knew only as wanting to cry and needing to *force* it. Being a great fan of Eugene Field at age seven and eight, I had learned that a child's death can guarantee total sadness, and I followed from there. ✍

THE NIGHT SANTA FAILED TO COME

by Jill Collins McCorkle

(1 9 6 5 ,   A G E   7)

Collins is McCorkle's mother's maiden name. Family names still hold significance for the author, who humorously presents two-time-divorcée Cindy, in Tending to Virginia, *as Cindy Sinclair Snipes Sinclair Biggers Sinclair.*

Santa looked very sad and said to his wife, Rudolph is no where in sight. What can I do? I don't know, said his wife that is a problem. I just can't go tomorrow night then. It was a real foggy night. Santa told the deers and elves that they could not go. Then a little elf, named Doppy, said, "why can't we have a search party." "O-K," said Santa. But they could not find him. Then Christmas night at 7:00 no Rudolph. 12:00 no Rudolph. It was the night after Christmas no Rudolph at all. Then Rudolph ran in and said, "Santa, I heard you before Christmas eve say I can't go." "Oh Rudolph I could not go because I did not have you." "Well Santa its O-K. Look" in ran all the children from different lands—Texas, Lumberton, the Northpole and every where. "Rudolph where are your shoes?" "I lost them. May I have some for Christmas?" "Yes you can, Rudolph." Come on boys and girls get your toys and candy. Then they went home and said thank you. Then Rudolph told them about it. After that Rudolph was always on time and one time he came in July. He saw some cotten plants and thought it was snow but if he did come to early sometimes He was always there on Christmas night all so.

MY FUNNY DREAMS
(1 9 6 5 ,   AGE   7)

"Lordy, someone Freudian would have a time with these!!" notes the author. In contrast to her sexually repressed cousin Virginia (Tending to Virginia), Cindy appears more in touch with her id. She hooks up with "wild raring stud" Buzz Biggers, a regrettable move that she blames on sexual hunger after her divorce, or on her shrink, or on "whoever said, 'if you fall off a horse you got to get back up and ride.'"

One night when I went to bed I dreamed a funny thing. I went down to my grandmas and there was a white horse. He was a little wild. But I got on him and then I wanted him. But I woke up. I had another dream one night now listen to this one. I had a big slinkey I opened it up and there right in front of me was a H-O-R-S-E and I closed the slinkey and the horse was gone. But I always wake up in no time. But I think I am always dreaming about some kind of horse. Some made out of slinkeys and some wild. But I had rather dream horses then any thing else.

SLINKEY or not.

D R E A M S

(1965, AGE 7)

Dreams take you far away over beams of light at night over a rain bow far away till you find the pot of gold you'v looked for all day at play. Dreams are funny don't you think some of a bunny licking honey. But you always wake up when it just got good of some thing like robin hood.

THE TWINS

(1966, AGE 8)

There once were a set of twins that were happy all day long. Whenever the other was gone, the other was right along. Then one day the little boy got an evil sickness and died. The little girl she cried, when she had lost her twin. She wouldn't eat. She wouldn't play until she was frail and thin. Then early one morn she was put out of misery and pain. And in the heavens there she lived with her brother once again.

In the morn there was a note by her bed that said, "Take & keep" and under it there was a butterfly that was dead. There was a flower from the springtime and a tear that she had shed.

Reacting to the loss of ☞ her husband, Sandra drops too much weight in the story "Crash Diet" (1987). She checks into the hospital, where "they just put me in a bed and gave me some dinner in my vein. . . ."

Jill McCorkle at age 8, holding her muse Shon-Ton. The author's writing place stands in the background.

In Tending to Virginia, *Emily chides Lena for having fed cats "better than people." Lena counters: "Because they're better than most people."*

SHON-TON
(1966, AGE 8)

I know a cat whose name is Shon-Ton. His fur is Black and White. He's always having lots of fun and going off at night. And when he gets the chance—straight into the house he will prance. Don't ask me why I watch this cat or how I have the time. I'll tell you right this minute because that cat is mine.

Jill McCorkle

Norman Mailer at about age 10, dressed for a costume party

norman mailer

ORMAN MAILER, WHO WAS once, as he has reluctantly
described himself, a "nice Jewish boy from Brooklyn," has
grown into one of America's most prominent literary celebrities.
He has attracted attention since early childhood, when, according to his
mother, as quoted in the Peter Manso biography, the family treated him
"'like he was a little god.'"

According to the same account, Mailer's IQ, clocked at 165, was announced by the principal at Mailer's eighth-grade graduation. When his
father sometimes complained about the mess in Norman's room, his mother
would counter presciently: "Leave him alone. He's going to be a great man."

"Before I was seventeen I had formed the desire to be a major writer,"
Mailer recalls in *Advertisements for Myself* (1959). At Harvard he began a
long stream of apprentice fiction, much of it in the style of Hemingway.

In 1948 at the age of twenty-five, he achieved instant fame with his war
novel *The Naked and the Dead*. Soon labeled an *enfant terrible*, Mailer was
launched on a roller-coaster career. The high points have included his
account of the 1967 March on the Pentagon, *Armies of the Night* (1968),
and his "true life novel" about Gary Gilmore, *The Executioner's Song*
(1979)—both Pulitzer Prize winners; his Egyptian novel, *Ancient Evenings*
(1983); and, in 1991, *Harlot's Ghost*, the first half of his "mega-novel" about
the CIA.

Even as a child, the author operated on a grand scale. The full version of "The Martian Invasion"—most of which, alas, is discouragingly buried in family storage—reaches 35,000 words. The childhood piece that follows is precocious in its prose and is an early foray into Mailer's ongoing exploration of masculine terrain but doesn't quite anticipate his roles as literary philosopher and cultural provocateur. ✑

THE MARTIAN INVASION

(1933, AGE 10)

Wanted for court martial and murder and hated by both sides, Captain Bob Porter and Private Ben Stein played their lone hand.

Chapter XI. A Mystery

The captives were placed in a prison for several days in which they were brutally treated by their captors.

Bob had a hard time restraining his temper. It was lucky for him he didn't as they might have killed him.

The next day they were chained onto the wall in the back part of a rocket boat. Bob knew in a hazy way that they were going towards the south in which there were the best places in the city. Among them was a huge castle that was crumbling to pieces.

Bob gave a sigh of relief that they were alone. The sigh turned into a groan as a pointed piece of iron fell onto Bob's arm. Bob saw that the edge was very sharp. Putting his teeth on it he started sawing at the chains. For a half hour he sawed at it before it broke.

Bob dropped the chains and took the piece of iron out of his sore and bleeding mouth. In an instant he was free. He then loosened the others bonds.

The captives then ranged on the front door. Bob then hit the metal door with a chain. The jailors came running over and opening the door rushed in. The Martians hadn't a chance. As each one came in he was knocked over the head until not one was left. The captives then ran through the open door locking it behind them.

Recalling the inspirations for "The Martian Invasion," Mailer told Vanity Fair: "I'd been listening to Buck Rogers on radio all winter. So that summer I wrote about my hero, Bob Porter. And there was a Dr. Huer—the origin of Hugh Montague in Harlot's Ghost."

In Advertisements for Myself, Mailer explains his pride over some of his adult fights: "I was a physical coward as a child."

Harlot's Ghost narrator Harry Hubbard fears and reveres his mentor Hugh Montague, a.k.a. Harlot. "He had not only been my boss, but my master in the only spiritual art that American men and boys respect—machismo."

Mailer's mother was so doting that, the author wrote in a 1991 magazine article, "If I had gone to the top of a tower in Texas and shot down seventeen people with a rifle, my mother would have said, 'Whatever did they do to make Norman so upset?'"

They then rushed up on the pilots who met the same fate—all except one who jumping out swam towards shore.

In an instant the alarm was given and a dozen boats rushed over to easily capture the boat.

Two hours later they were again bound and guarded in a new rocket ship as the old one was demolished. They were rushed out and were herded into a small passage that led into a huge round ball building that had no windows.

They were ushered into a room where they were blindfolded and taken through so many corridors and rooms that they hadn't an inkling at the end of where they had went. Finally they were made to descend eighty steps. Bob counted them. They were then bound on their hands and arms. The guard then took a rope rolling it over them, then he fastened them to the floor with ropes.

The captives waited half an hour before they heard a thing, but when they did they wished they hadn't. A fearful laugh sounded all through the room. Then a part of the ceiling slowly began to move towards the floor. On it was a big Martian who with a big stick kept hitting it on his chair making an eerie sound.

Then to the surprise of all he said, "Welcome friends to our country." Bob gasped in amazement and the thought ran through his mind how did he know English.

The Martian reading his thoughts laughed and said, "My friend wants to know how I speak english." Bob noticed that he was purple with laughter.

Bob had noticed that the man talked with a French accent. Bob had a smattering of French so he said, "Parlez vous Francaise." The Marsian answered, "Oui, oui, mons—you dog," he shouted, "the idea."

Bob lay back choking his laughter back. The Martian sputtered in rage and threw his scepter at him. Bob dodged it and it fell on the ground after hitting the wall.

Then he continued, "You shall die a nice death, a very nice death." The Martian again became purple. He then said, "Suffocation is nice isn't it. A slow long drawn out death, ho, ho, ho, ho, ho." And again the monster laughed.

Bob felt an eerie chilling of his veins and his heart seemed dead. How he wished he was loose and had an electric pistol.

The Martian calmly continued, "Do not try to escape as you would never get away. You will be fed but don't be happy, you haven't a chance. As for you, you silly dumbbell who thinks he is smarter than I, you shall not get anything to eat and the jailors will do so much that you will be sorry. Remember all of you that death comes five days from now." Saying these words he left the chamber letting the captives ponder over their fate.

Mailer returns for some more French mischief by having DJ, the scatological 🖎 narrator of Why Are We in Vietnam? *blurt out:*

"Oo la la, Françoise, your trou de merde is inoubliable for it is like the Camembert my mozzaire used to make when we were young, Boonkie."

"They were going to beat him up, because they had not been as smart as he. It was not fair," thinks Al Groot, the teen hero of Mailer's story "The Greatest Thing in the World," written when he 🖎 was age 18. It won first prize in Story *magazine's 1941 college contest, giving Mailer vital encouragement.*

Norman Mailer

Joyce Carol Oates at age 20

joyce carol oates

"M Y CHILDHOOD SEEMS TO have been plowed under, gone subterranean as a dream," writes Joyce Carol Oates about the small New York farm, now gone, where she grew up. In a loving essay about her parents, Oates recalls the family fruit orchard, chickens pecking in the dirt, and the thrill of flying, very young, with her father in a two-seat airplane.

Other accounts describe a grim cast to her childhood, due in part to the depressed, backward nature of the region outside Lockport, New York (where she was born in 1938). "A great deal frightened me," she once told an interviewer without elaborating.

In elementary school, during the late 1940s and early 1950s, she attended a single-room schoolhouse, where one teacher was responsible for eight grades. Nonetheless, by her early teens Oates was reading Faulkner, Dostoevsky, Thoreau, and many other literary giants. She was also an eager writer, who sent out her first novel at age fifteen. About a drug addict who finds rehabilitation in a black stallion, the manuscript was rejected as too depressing for young readers. She practiced, during high school, "by writing novel after novel and always throwing them out when I completed them." A scholarship recipient at the University of Syracuse, "she was the most brilliant student we've ever had here," said Professor Donald A. Dike in 1972. He recalled that Oates wrote mostly short stories, "but about once a term she'd drop a 400-page novel on my desk and I'd read that, too.

She had some conscience problems about her writing in those days; she was afraid it was 'not nice' and might offend her parents, and I tried to reassure her."

Oates continues to be one of our most prolific authors, having published more than seventy-five volumes of fiction, poetry, drama, and essays. The novels *Them* (1969), *Wonderland* (1971), and *Bellefleur* (1980) are among the best known of her works.

She writes, in part, about the "harsh and unsentimental world" that shaped her parents' lives, a world that includes the Great Depression and abandonment (her father's father had once run off, and her mother had been put up for adoption as an infant after *her* father was killed in a tavern brawl). Oates's characters often lack a complete sense of self, harbor a cautious yearning, remember or repress a strained or hurtful family life, and cope with unpredictable surges of violence.

In her teenage story that follows (first published in her high school magazine), Oates experiments with elements that resurface in her adult work: the unappreciated child, the frightening parent, the pull and push of "home," the fragility of family bonds, and the power of memory to strengthen or diminish those bonds. Though Oates's work is concerned with a range of social issues, the emotional core is often familial: "A father, a mother, a few beloved people—" she told interviewer Joe David Bellamy in 1972, "that is the extent of the universe, emotionally." ∅

A LONG WAY HOME

by Joyce Oates

(1 9 5 6 ,   a g e   1 7)

I can still remember the day Albie came home from the war. I can still remember how happy everybody was and how nice things were at our house while we were waiting for him. You might think that I was too young at the time to remember anything that happened so long ago, but when something very important happens it is often more difficult to forget than to remember.

When I got up, I could tell right away that the day was something special. Downstairs everything was clean and shiny and had a fresh, out-of-doors sort of smell, and there were flowers on the table—red, dark red, real dark red roses that Mom had picked from out along the fence. Some new yellow curtains, that she had been making for a long time, were up in the kitchen, and I could smell the warm, sweet smell of pie baking. The minute I went into the kitchen and saw Mom I remembered why everything was so different and so nice—today was the day Albie was coming home.

It is not uncommon for Oates to write from the point of view of male characters. She is as sympathetic with any of them as with her female characters, according to her response to one interviewer. "In many respects," she said, "I am closest in temperament to certain of my male characters."

"Good morning, Jack!" my mother said. She was smiling and looked very happy.

"'Morning," I said.

"And did you have a good night's sleep?"

She had never before asked me this question, and I did not know exactly how to answer it. I said: "Okay, I guess," but I don't think she was listening. She was doing something else, and saying:

"Do you know where your father is?"

"No."

"He's gone down to the station."

"Huh?"

"The railroad station," she said. She took out a pie and put it on the window sill, holding it carefully with potholders so she would not burn her hands.

"The railroad station is where the trains come in, Jack."

"Oh, like in the movie we saw last week!"

"Yes, Jack, yes, you're right!" She looked very happy and even smiled at me instead of scolding me for being stupid as she sometimes did. "You're absolutely right! Oh, Jack, isn't it just wonderful?"

"You mean Albie coming home?"

"Why, of course! What else could I mean?" She went to the window and looked out at the road. "You don't know how afraid I've been, all these months. Thinking—just thinking, and not being able to do anything—sitting home here and just thinking and worrying about him . . . so far away. But now he's here! He's why, he's within the state already, and he's coming this way. He's coming home."

"Will we go fishing again?" I asked.

"Not today."

"I want to go fishing today."

"No, no, you can't! Today is something special; your brother is coming home," she said. She was not looking at me. "You have to be dressed nicely and be very nice to him and make things as nice here as possible, so he will realize how valuable his home is. Out on the battlefield, away from his parents and his home, a boy might begin to forget . . . but not Albie."

"Maybe we can go fishing tomorrow."

"His letters were so short, and some of them didn't come for so long," she went on slowly. "And sometimes . . . Well, they must have been lost in the mails; the mails here are so bad, and of course across

One by one, family members leave or die and are replaced and soon forgotten in Oates's dystopian short story "Family" (1989). As they huddle together against their toxic world, the family members also struggle with their own failing memories—memory being, the story suggests, the necessary fixative of love. ☞

the ocean the mail service is absolutely terrible . . . everybody knows that."

"Wait till he sees how I painted the boat," I said.

"He'll love it here. Everything is fixed up for him. I've made a pie and we're having chicken for supper and everything is just going to be wonderful. Compared to what he's been through . . . he'll love it here."

"When will he be here?"

"What, Jack? What did you say?"

"When will he get here?"

"In about an hour." She turned and looked at me with a smile, but it faded from her face when she saw me. "Jack! I told you last night to put on your new shirt and trousers this morning!"

"But I'm going fishing afterward, and you always tell me to wear my jeans . . ."

"Can't you understand? Can't you understand that today is something special?" she asked. She was getting angry, and I did not want to be hit. "Your brother is coming home. Albie is coming home. Can't you understand that—don't you have any feelings at all?"

"I'm sorry," I said again.

"Oh, you're not really. You're not; you know it, you just deliberately forgot about it," she said. "You do anything to make me angry, when you know what headaches it gives me."

"I'm sorry," I said. "I'll put the other things on." I went out of the kitchen and back upstairs and changed my clothes, and this time I did not come back down again.

I sat by my window and looked out, and it was a beautiful day. There were birds in the tree outside

---

". . . Daddy . . . hit me. I don't . . . know why. I . . . don't know if I was bad." So 11-year-old Kathleen Hennessy, in The Rise of Life on Earth (1991), *describes her bewilderment and lack of control, conditions often familiar to Oates's fictional* ☞ *children.*

Many of Oates's characters learn to withdraw from upsetting situations. Joy, for example, in "The Seasons" (1983), when asked if her abortion was painless, immediately responds that ☞ *she can't remember.*

the window, and they all seemed very happy, and everything was perfect. It was a good day for fishing, and I could not understand why Albie would not want to go. He always loved fishing, and I should have thought it would be the first thing he would want to do. It would be for me.

I looked at Albie's bed. Mom had made a new bedspread for it, a pretty blue one that was a lot prettier than my grey one. Albie ought to like it, she said, because it was so gay and pretty and he would want things to be gay and pretty after the war and everything. I did not know what she meant by everything, but when I asked her she just said that she did not know herself, and so I forgot about it. Up on the wall was the football letter Albie had got in high school. He had been wonderful; Mom told me he had been captain of the football team and in every activity at school and one of the most popular boys. She only wished that I would be like him, but she said that it did not look as though I would. It was funny, but I did not remember any of these things about Albie. I did not remember him in football games although I know I went to many of them. I did not remember him as sitting around home and being so nice and polite and helping with all the work as Mom told me he was, and as Mom told me I ought to try to be. I remembered Albie only as an almost faceless, pleasant boy who went fishing with me and even let me row sometimes. I remembered that he smiled a lot when we were outside and that he was very nice, while my friend Bill's big brother would always chase us and never was nice to us at all. I remembered how we would talk late into the night about

In Oates's story "Where Are You Going, Where Have You Been?" (1966), Connie's older sister June gets all their mother's praise. "June did this, June did that . . . and Connie couldn't do a thing, her mind was all filled with trashy daydreams." ☞

things, about Christmas and Halloween and school and how he would take care of any of the big boys who acted tough with me when I went to school on the first day. I remembered sled riding in winter and running out on the ice on the creek, and I remembered fishing again, and being taught how to pitch although I was really too young to be able to throw hard.

Her own bus ride to school was filled with rough, bullying kids, recalled Oates in a 1980 profile. "It was exhausting. A continual daily scramble for existence." "You hypnotize yourself

I remembered Albie sitting with the big boys in the back of the bus; I remembered being proud and glad that he was as good as any of them and that he even talked to me once in a while when we were on the school bus. I remembered the day he went away with the suitcases and how everybody had gone along with him to the "station" and I had been left home with my sister, Ann, and how they had all come home very sad and were mad at me for any little thing I did. I remembered all these things although I did not even have to try, and although I did not even know that I knew them. They all came back just like that, and it made me glad to know that Albie was coming home after so long.

Later on I saw the car come into the driveway, and I went downstairs. My mother had run outside and had even let the screen door slam, so I did the same thing. I felt terribly happy and I looked to see if everyone else felt the same way so I would not be scolded or anything, and they all looked happy too and so I did not have to worry. My sister Ann and my mother and my aunt Alma were all out by the car. They were very happy, putting their arms around

Albie's neck and kissing him and saying how glad they were that he was back, and how wonderful it was to see him again. Dad, too, was very happy although he stood back and let my mother and aunt and sister talk as much as they wanted. I went up to the car to get a look at him; it had been so long since I had seen him last. Now that I got closer I felt almost sad, because I did not know what I could say to him, and I suddenly had the idea that maybe he was grown up now and like my father and mother.

"Where's Jack? Hey, where's Jack? Oh, there he is—! Hi, Jack," Albie said.

"Hi," I said.

"You don't look very happy," Albie said. He was smiling in a funny way, and I could see that he was not the same. It made me feel all the sadder, because I had never thought that when Albie went away that he would not come back Albie again.

"I wanted to go fishing with you," I said.

"Jack!" my mother said. She was surprised and angry.

Albie looked over toward the creek. "I've been thinking about fishing," he said. "I've been thinking about it a lot."

"I go almost every day," I said.

"Who do you go with?"

"Oh, Bill, now."

"Do you catch much?"

"No."

He looked around at the tear-stained faces of my mother and sister and aunt. "We'll go sometime, you and I," he said. "You don't know how I've been thinking about it."

"About fish?" I asked. "About the twenty-incher you got that time?"

"No, not about fish," he said. "Just about the creek and how we would go rowing on it, trolling at night."

"But we never caught much then."

"Oh, you two!" Mom said suddenly, dabbing at her eyes with a handkerchief. "Talking about fishing, and at a time like this! Oh, Albie, you don't know how wonderful it is to see you again—! But I must get a grip on myself, I must calm down. As you can see, Albie, since you went away, I'm not . . . I'm not very—*well.*"

My aunt Alma put her hand on Mom's arm and said: "Now you just come inside. We'll all go inside and talk about things, and then it will be about time for lunch. Wouldn't you like that? Now, of course, you would.—You've gotten thinner, Albie, I do declare! We'll have to put some more of that fat back on you, won't we? My, how thin your face is!"

Albie brought his things into the house and put them upstairs in his room, and when he came down again we all sat in the living room and talked. My mother had very much to tell him, although I cannot remember any of it now. My father told him something about a job waiting for him, a good job and a place in the union, too, and how they were always looking for good men. My aunt told him some things about the family, about old Uncle Pete who had died last winter and how he had suffered at the end, and about Martha, who had had that terrible three hour operation, and about her own troubles that she was having with her heart—or she thought it was her heart. My sister Ann told him about some girl named Cindy that he apparently had known, because he was interested for a while. My sister said something about the girl coming over for dinner that night, but then Albie had stopped smiling. He did not look well.

"I saw Cindy the other day in town," Mom said. She was still dabbing at her eyes although she did not seem to be crying any longer. "Just the other day, in front of the bakery. Of course she knows all about your coming home, probably even knew about it before I did; I wouldn't doubt it any—! And we were both so excited; we were both so happy—! Why, even now I can hardly believe that—"

"It's all fixed up with this man, this Morgan, I was telling you about," Dad said. "You'll start in sort of low, of course, but pretty high compared to what you'd get in any other job. Like I said, they're looking for bright young men these days. Got to have bright young men to keep industry going. Union looking for 'em too. You're in, solid, and let me tell you that being my son might have just a little bit to do with it." He laughed and offered Albie a cigarette, which he took and lit for himself. "Yessir, just a little bit to do with it! You don't know how good it makes a man feel to be able to help his son out."

"Do you suppose you and Cindy will be getting married now?" my mother asked. "Such a lovely, wonderful child that girl is! Of course, both of you are young, so terribly young, but it would be so nice . . . She thinks the world of you, Albie, just like we all do!"

"And about transportation, son. There won't be any fooling around with buses or anything. You'll get a ride with some guys I know who go right by the plant—Al Robinson and Steve Martin. You know them, don't you? Sure you do, you used to go and watch me bowl and they were on my team. Well, you'll get a ride with them and there won't be any fooling around with buses—late half the time and so far to walk to anyway. Things are all planned. It'll be just like it would have been if you'd never even left."

"Cindy's coming over tonight. Did Ann tell you? Oh, Albie, I've made the most wonderful dinner for us—I can't wait till you taste it! It's so wonderful to have you back again, to see you . . . You know, you haven't changed a bit, not a single tiny bit! You're still my Albie, my little Albie . . . oh, thank God you're here with us and safe!"

into loving your life because it's what you are doing and because it's life," complains Kim in Oates's story "House Hunting" (1987). Albie seems similarly disinclined to be mesmerized by the routine existence his parents propose.

In "House

Albie looked away from her and kept on smoking the cigarette. I did not remember that he smoked, but somehow it did not surprise me. He wasn't Albie. He wasn't the boy I remembered, the boy with whom I had gone fishing and fought and talked and gotten into trouble. He was somebody else. I did not know this somebody else, and I did not dislike this somebody else, but I wanted to like him very much and I felt very sorry for him. I just kept staring and did not say a thing.

Albie looked at me and said:

"Maybe you're thinking you won't be wanting to share a room with me."

"No," I said. "I don't mind."

"Of course he doesn't," my mother said sharply. "He certainly doesn't—"

"Did you miss me, Jack?" he asked.

I did not know what to say. "Yes," I said after a moment. "I missed you at first because it was so lonely at night, and I didn't have anyone to go out on the creek with."

"And then—?"

"I sort of forgot after a while."

"That's good, Jack."

"Why, you terrible little brat!" my mother said. "Did you hear him, Harry? Did you hear what that boy said—to his own brother?"

"I'm sorry if it's wrong," I said. I was becoming afraid. I thought she might hit me. "I'm sorry, I really am!"

"Don't pay any attention to him," my father said. He was angry. "Go outside, Jack. Go outside and play with Bill. Go fishing—go on."

"Change your clothes first," my mother said.

When I had gone as far as the doorway, I heard Albie say:

"I'm going to go with him."

"But, Albie, we have so much to talk about . . ."

"I know he didn't mean what he said; he's so little. Think when you were his age!"

"I want to go out with him," Albie said. He had not finished his cigarette but he put it out in an ash tray.

"Albie," my mother said. She began to cry again. "Don't you want to talk to us? Don't you want to tell us everything that you did?"

"No," he said.

She wiped her eyes. "Albie, dear! Don't you see how everything is fixed up for you? Don't you see how pretty everything is?"

"Nothing's pretty," he said.

My mother got up. "Look at these curtains, Albie! Just look at them! Why, I worked for hours and hours to get them done in time for your homecoming, just for *you*. Don't you think they're beautiful? Would you like some in your room, maybe? I could make them if you wanted—"

"I don't want any in my room," he said.

My mother went to the table. "Look at the beautiful roses I picked! They're growing out along the fence yet, the same kind you used to pick me when you were Jack's age . . . Aren't they beautiful, Albie? Don't you think they're beautiful?"

"They're red," he said. He looked sick. "I hate red."

"Albie, is something wrong with you?" my mother asked. She went to him and tried to put her arms around his neck, but he would have none of it. "What's wrong? Can't you tell me? Don't you see how we've fixed everything up for you? Can't you smell the pie and the flowers, and everything—all for you?"

He would not answer, and she went on, trying to smile as though she thought herself silly: "Albie, you just can't imagine all the days and nights I've worried about you . . . all the things I knitted to send to you, and all the letters I wrote . . . Can't you say thank you? Can't you tell me you were glad to get them?" She could not smile any longer and said in a fast, shaking, almost hysterical voice: "The scarf! The one with your initials on it, in your favorite color blue! Didn't it keep you warm out there? Why didn't you ever say thank you for it? Can't you say thank you now?"

He turned away and did not answer.

She took hold of his arm. "I don't understand what's wrong with you."

Hunting," *a matronly real estate agent tries to coax Joel Collier into the purchase of a home. But Joel, traumatized by the loss of his baby, is as alienated from her as postwar Albie is from his family.*

He kept looking out the window. He said nothing, and I felt sorry for him because I knew he had nothing to say, in the same way that I no longer had anything to say to him.

"Albie, you act as though you don't love us! You act as though you—don't even know us anymore!"

She clutched at his arm, grabbing the dull khaki cloth. "Can't you say anything? What's wrong?—You're tired; that's what it is; you're tired and hungry and—Just go along now and change your clothes, and after you've eaten everything will be all right, everything will be just the way it was before—"

Home also presents problems for the teenage narrator of Oates's 1969 story "How I Contemplated the World from the Detroit House of Correction and Began My Life over Again." She is emotionally disconnected from her parents' comfortable, but oblivious, suburban lives and flees into a nightmarish skid row adventure. Even after she returns, the reconciliation she forges with her surroundings is an uneasy one. ". . . I love everything here . . . ," she concludes, somewhat hysterically. "I am home."

"But it won't!" Albie said. He pulled his arm away from her slowly, almost reluctantly. "You don't understand," he said, as though he himself did not understand either. "It won't be the same."

They looked at each other. My mother said: "What . . . won't be the same?"

"I don't know," said Albie. He was trying not to hurt her, but it was a difficult thing to do. "It's something you . . . can't understand."

"Albie—what—where are you going?"

"I don't know yet," he said, "but I have to leave."

"You can't, you just came home!"

"I have to leave," he said. "I can't stay here. I'm sorry, but I can't stay here." He felt bad about this, but he knew it had to be done, and he was trying not to hurt her. He was really trying his best not to hurt her.

They stared at him in silence. He left the living room and went upstairs, and when he came down again he was carrying his suitcases. He went right on outside again, not looking toward us, and they hurried out after him.

I went back up to my room. It was all mine now, but I realized that it had been all mine for a long time. I sat for a while on the other bed and felt the pretty blue bedspread and even got it a little dirty from my shoes. After a while I got up and took down the big football letter. It had been getting dusty on the wall and I knew that, underneath my shirts in the drawer, it would be much easier to forget about.

Joyce Carol Oates

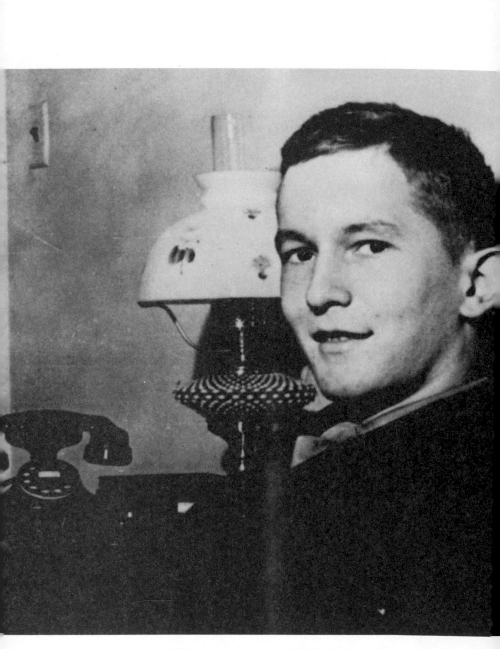

William Styron at age 18, U.S. Marine Corps, Newport News, Va.

william styron

WILLIAM STYRON WAS FIRST exposed to books when, as a small child, he served as his mother's courier to and from the local lending library. Bedridden with illness for much of her life, she died when Styron was age thirteen; the loss would affect, the author says, his own depressive illness, as well as, at least one scholar notes, the dark vision explored in Styron's fiction.

Styron himself had almost died the year before when the small boat he was sailing capsized and sank into the James River of his native Tidewater, Virginia. This region, where Styron was born in 1925, figures prominently in such novels as *Lie Down in Darkness* (1951) and *The Confessions of Nat Turner* (1967). The near-drowning episode is fictionalized in his 1959 novel *Set This House on Fire*. With this incident, the narrator recalls, "there had been taken away from me that child's notion that I would live forever."

War and its losses would also influence Styron's literary vision, as demonstrated most strikingly in his 1979 novel *Sophie's Choice*. But during his high school years, Styron was eager to "taste the glory of military life," he writes in his collection of nonfiction *This Quiet Dust and Other Writings* (1982). While a student at Davidson College, Styron wrote the following satire, which mocks the hypocrisy he saw in his college administration's efforts to keep him out of military service. He explains:

> Students were being implored by many college administra-
> tions to remain in school (if the students were male) and get as

much ("get all you can") education as possible before going into the service. In addition, at Davidson, the Army Air Corps [A.A.C.] had established a student training program, which caused an incredible amount of congestion as the original Davidson students found themselves being crowded out by the A.A.C. enlistees. This inevitably led to the suspicion (conviction, really) that the college was trying to have it both ways financially —getting money both from the students and Uncle Sam.

Displaying a "strain of suicidal bravado," Styron left Davidson that same spring of 1943, at the tender age of seventeen, to join the Marine Corps. Before long he would train his satirical eye on the armed services themselves.

"When I was quite young," recalls the author, "and in school, or later in the Marine Corps, I realized how powerfully I was repelled by authority." ℘

GET ALL YOU CAN
A *parody in verse*
by Bill Styron
(1943, AGE 17)

Styron is "almost ☞ certain" that he wrote this prefatory Editor's Note.

(Editor's note: During the past year numerous talks have been made by our President, Dr. Cunningham, on the expediency of remaining in school and obtaining the full benefit of Davidson's educational facilities before entering the Armed Forces. We believe that the policy which the administration has followed in advising students has been wise, and it is evident that the interest of the Davidson students has been foremost in the minds of Dr. Cunningham and the other members of the faculty. The advice to each individual has been wholly unselfish on the part of the college, and the withdrawal of a number of students is the result of conditions beyond the control of the college or the students. The verse on the next few pages does not intimate mercenary tendencies within the administration, far from that, but it is simply the author's perversion of some of the facts in order to create an extremely satire-able situation.)

Coleridge
The Rhyme of the Ancient Mariner
It is a College President,
And much surprised are we;
"By that tailored suit and Arrow tie,
What shalt thou say to me?"

He holds us with his faultless voice,
"Get all you can," quoth he;
Speak on, speak on, O President,
Eftsoons with smiles spake he.   Eftsoons: *at once*

The students all sat in their seats:
They cannot choose but listen;
And as he spake in flowing words,   *Nathan, in* Sophie's
Their eyes, behold did glisten.   Choice, *is a talented*
                                                            caricaturist: ". . . his gift
                                                            was not mimicry alone;
"I urge of you emphatically   *what emanated from him*
To stay in school," he cried;   *so drolly was the product*
"You shall be here quite long, you see;"   *of dazzling invention," the*
Forsooth the students sighed.   *narrator, Stingo, tells us,*
                                                            referring to Nathan's
Day after day, day after day   *southern impersonations.*
We stayed, and had no notion

The V-1 would call us, yea,
To sail upon the ocean.

Army, Navy, everywhere
The students all did shrink,
Evacuate both East and West;
Morale began to sink.

Fill up that dormitory room
With five, or six, or more;

E.R.C.: ☞
Enlisted Reserve Corps

There goes a man to the E.R.C.,
Which leaves us now but four

The President, whose eye is bright,
And said "get all you can and more,"
Is gone and now the College Stud
Turned from Dean Bailey's door.

He went like one that hath been stunned
And is of sense forlorn,
A sadder and a drafted man,
He left last Tuesday morn.

Shakespeare

Hamlet Soliloquizing

In Styron's story ☞
*"Love Day" (1985), Lieu-
tenant Stiles mocks a
"sham" decoy invasion, on
which he has been ordered,
by performing his King
Harry impression, holler-
ing out lines from* Henry
V *to his amused troops.*

To be or not to be: 'tis not the question;
But whether 'tis nobler to suffer the stress and strain
    of six more months,
Or to take arms like any other draftee
And end up a buck private. The E.R.C.,
No more; and by the E.R.C. to say
We end the deals and extended operations
The flesh is heir to, 'tis a consummation

Completely to be avoided. Get all you can;
All; perchance some more; ay, there's the J.O.;
For in that sleep of death called education
What things may come when we
Have shuffled off for the week-end,
Must give us pause: there's the respect
That makes calamity of a Phi Bete average;
But what limber would bear
The whips and scorns of a top sergeant
When he himself might a dealer make
With a bare bottle? Atch!

Kipling

Tommy Atkins

I went to Monday's Chapel talk to see wot I could
    see;
Cunningham 'e up an' sez, "They've called the
    E.R.C."
The faculty behin' their doors they laughed an'
    giggled fit to die,
I ousts right over to my room
    and to myself sez I:
O it's students this an' students that
    an' "we'll draft yer jus' the same,"
But it was "Thank yer, Mister Student,"
    before the Air Corps came,
Before the Air Corps came, my boys,
    before the Air Corps came,
O it was "Thank yer, Mister Student,"
    before the Air Corps came.

I went to Jackson's house one day, as meek as I
    could be,
'E sez to me, "Git out o' West, 'ere comes the A.A.C.;

"Only one English poet escaped being a pederast, and that was Kipling," pronounces Captain Budwinkle, an insipid military functionary in Styron's 1972 satirical play In the Clap Shack. *Budwinkle then recites his favorite lines: "But the head and the hoof of the Law / and the haunch and the hump / is—Obey!"*

In Styron's novel *The Long March (1952)*, Captain Mannix focuses his "disgruntled sense of humor" on the marine reserves when he finds himself back in boot camp. "Corporal, kindly pass out the atom bombs for inspection," he quips, in parody of the tedious, banal lectures on military doctrine he is forced to attend.

Move yer things, pack yer stuff,
    you ain't got long to stay;
Find a place somewheres in town,
    you're drafted anyway!"
And it's students this an' students that,
    an' "students go away;"
But it was "we love yer, Mister Student,"
    before the Air Corps' stay,
Before the Air Corps' stay, my boys,
    before the Air Corps' stay,
O 'twas "we love yer Mister Student,"
    before the Air Corps' stay.

Tennyson
Charge of the Light Brigade

Half a year, half a year,
Half a year onward,
Into the E.R.C.
There were 600 students at Davidson in 1942 (before the influx brought about by the A.A.C.), the author explains.
Went the Six Hundred;
"Stay here, get all you can,
We're with you, man for man,
You'll never see Japan!"
    Blissful Six Hundred.

Then came the A.A.C.,
Can there some changes be?
Not though the students knew
Someone had blundered.
Theirs not to reason why
From East they quickly fly,

"No refund!" comes Jackson's cry.
      Crowded Six Hundred.

Army to right of them,
Navy to left of them,
4-F beyond them,
      All of them thundered.
"This room will hold four,
In a pinch, perhaps more,
Sleep there on the floor!"
      Dwindling Six Hundred.

When will their memory fade?
O what a sight they made!
      Nobody wondered.
Most are now gone for good,
They got all they could,
      Noble Six Hundred.

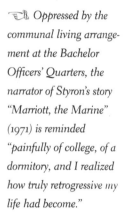 *Oppressed by the communal living arrangement at the Bachelor Officers' Quarters, the narrator of Styron's story "Marriott, the Marine" (1971) is reminded "painfully of college, of a dormitory, and I realized how truly retrogressive my life had become."*

William Styron

Amy Tan at age 8. "Each morning before school," says Tan's character Waverly Jong in *The Joy Luck Club*, "my mother would twist and yank on my thick black hair until she had formed two tightly wound pigtails."

a m y
t a n

I N AMY TAN'S WILDLY successful first book *The Joy Luck Club* (1989), four Chinese-born mothers try to share their personal and cultural heritage with their four American-born daughters. One daughter, Jing-mei "June" Woo, responds to her mother's death by going to China to look for family there. Central to this collection of interrelated stories and to Tan's novels *The Kitchen God's Wife* (1991) and *The Hundred Secret Senses* (1996) is the significance of place—countries, cities, houses, landmarks—and its loss and discovery as well.

In the childhood essay that follows, Tan eulogizes one of her favorite haunts: the old public library building in Santa Rosa, California. As an eight-year-old, she wrote this tribute for a contest sponsored by a local citizens group. Her winning entry was published along with other children's themes on the same topic in the Santa Rosa *Press Democrat*.

Amy Tan remarks:

Upon re-reading this piece, "What the Library Means to Me," I am struck by the fact that my writing style has changed very little since I was eight years old. No doubt I was influenced by my father, a Baptist minister. And so I tried to be as direct and as honest as possible, writing the way I talked. I wrote about emotions, the basics, happiness and sadness. I already had a fondness for metaphors, and in fact, those doors and windows are still pretty much the way I feel about reading fiction today. And I also brought up, as did my father at the end of a sermon, a pitch for money cloaked in the example of my own charitable giving. Although nowhere in my wildest eight-year-old imagination did I ever dream I could one day sell a book. ✑

WHAT THE LIBRARY MEANS TO ME
(1961, AGE 8)

Tan picks up the architecture-of-the mind metaphor in The Joy Luck Club, *when Rose describes Old Mr. Chou, the guardian of dreams, as presiding over a door beyond which she finds herself in "a house without doors or windows."* ☞

My name is Amy Tan, 8 years old, a third grader in Matanzas School. It is a brand new school and everything is so nice and pretty. I love school because the many things I learn seem to turn on a light in the little room in my mind. I can see a lot of things I have never seen before. I can read many interesting books by myself now. I love to read. My father takes me to the library every two weeks, and I check five or six books each time. These books seem to open many windows in my little room. I can see many wonderful things outside. I always look forward to go the library.

Once my father did not take me to the library for a whole month. He said, the library was closed because the building is too old. I missed it like a good friend. It seems a long long time my father took me to the Library again just before Christmas. Now it is on the second floor of some stores. I wish we can have a real nice and pretty library like my school. I put 18 cents in the box and signed my name to join Citizens of Santa Rosa Library.

☜ Joy Luck's *Suyuan Woo returns to Shanghai in search of her family only to find that their house no longer exists. "I kept looking up to where the house used to be," she says. "And it wasn't a house, just the sky."*

Amy Tan

John Updike at about age 14 (at left, seated), with his Lutheran confirmation class.
"I'm the little blurry fellow sitting in the row with the girls," Updike points out.
"As you can see, I don't look happy."

john updike

J OHN UPDIKE'S SMALL-TOWN childhood—short on glamour but rich in the daily magic of place, thought, and human interaction—underlies many of his nearly fifty books of prose and poetry.

Born in 1932 in Shillington, Pennsylvania, Updike, an only child, took his boyhood pleasures passively, shyly—"burrowing in New York magazines and English mystery novels for the secret passageway out, the path of avoidance and vindication"—as he anticipated that day when he would do something worth admiring, something beyond his hometown's scope. And, in the bargain, he relates in his 1989 memoir *Self-Consciousness*, he would redress his father's meagerly rewarded career as a schoolteacher.

Updike confesses that one of the past selves that makes him cringe is the boy of 1945 to 1948: the boy who wrote the mystery novel that follows. His family had moved from Shillington to an eighty-acre farm eleven miles away, and this rural isolation imposed, until he was old enough to drive, feelings of awkwardness and exile. Avid reading provided his relief, as the young Updike continued to develop his "belief in print, in ink, in a sacred realm of publication," as he puts it in his memoir, that would "redeem" him.

He has managed to earn several million words' worth of redemption, beginning professionally with pieces for the *New Yorker*—to whose sophisticated pages Updike aspired since early adolescence—and continuing with such best-selling novels as *Couples* (1968), *The Witches of Eastwick* (1984), and *Toward the End of Time* (1997). Winner of most of the top literary prizes, Updike is best known for the famous Rabbit novels, which focus on a former high school basketball star—and the America around him—at different periods of his life.

Updike's partial mystery novel written at age fourteen prefigures his tremendous facility with language and his ambitious productivity, as well as an enduring fascination with misbehavior, befitting a boy with a "docile, good-child nature."

The author says of his contribution to this anthology:

> To my imperfect recollection, this was my first extended effort in fiction, except for some fables imitating Thurber's. It must have been composed in the summer, when I had the time; on the other side of one page is a poem signed "John Updike 8B," so I would place it in the summer between eighth and ninth grade, when I, with a March birthday, was fourteen years old. I had been a mystery-novel reader for some years—of Erle Stanley Gardner, Ellery Queen, Agatha Christie, John Dickson Carr.
>
> The frightful fallibility of the creative process is here naked —the misspellings, the character misplacements, the repeatedly slippery details. I recognize myself all too well in this pubescent per-petrator of dialogue, facial descriptions, and—very transparently —suspense. Seeking the clue-cluttered atmosphere of a classic detective puzzle, he created pure clutter and a glacial stasis of action.
>
> My editorial policy toward my struggling younger self has been that we should keep his misspellings, but where only a mis-take in typing is involved, it should be silently corrected. He seems to have worked in some haste, and with a sticky machine. ✑

UNTITLED MYSTERY

(CIRCA 1946, AGE 14)

My employer, Manuel Citarro, pushed the letter across the desk at me. It was written in a large, mascueline hand, with no curly-cues and a firm down-stroke. "Mr. Citarro," it read, "I would like your presence over the week-end at my country home, White Haven. There will be three other guests besides yourself. The visit may have some interest professionly to you. Let me know if you can come.

WALTER HALDEMAN"

"Doesn't waste ink, does he," I remarked.

"That is what makes it so interesting," Manuel replied. "It is more like a command than an invation. Not one please, in the entire letter. The "interest professionally" sentance is indeed fascenating. It might mean anything. His wife might be unfaithful, his butler might be a pilferer, his dog might have fits, or his life might be in danger."

I chuckled. "Probably one of the first three. A big man like Walt Haldeman imagines he has to have the best of everything for anything, no matter how trifling. He probably calls in Adrian when his little girl wants a new doll-dress made."

"He doesn't have a little girl. And I disagree with you. I sense something big, important here, regardless of his vague phraseology."

"Surely you're not going?"

"I am."

So it was that, later, Manuel Citarro, the famous detective and Thomas Mays, his obscure but deserving secretary, stepped off of a grimy little train unto a grimier little railroad station called "White Haven." It was the station that was named after the home of

After contemplating a childhood photo of himself, the adult Updike describes feeling like the phantom creation of the child's ambition to become an artist. "Now I wait apprehensively for his next command," he writes in "The Dogwood Tree: A Boyhood" (1962), "or at least a nod of appreciation, and he smiles through me, as if I am already transparent with failure."

☜ Gilbert Adrian (1903–59), Hollywood costume and set designer.

Walter Haldeman, and not the other way around. White Haven station is about 30 miles, or 45 minutes, from New York City. The home White Haven is a mile from the station.

"You must be Mr. Sitarro," a slackmouthed young man addressed himself to my employer. He pronounced the "C" like "S."

"Yes, I am Mr. Kitarro."

"I was told to pick ya' up." He threw me a nasty look.

"This is my secretary, Thomas Mays," Citarro intervened. "He is with me."

"I wasn't told there'd be nobody else," he growled. He didn't like me very much.

"Well, I'm sure it's quite all right," Citarro snapped, "I must have my secretary, I'm sure that my hostess will understand." Then he became mellow and kindly, laying a hand on my shoulder. "Mays, here, is as important to me as my right hand." He waggled his right hand. "I could not do without him." I think he did that mainly to embarres me, for it was not the truth. I had been with Citarro for only three weeks and I could not feel that I was very important to him. It was my task to read his commoner fan mail, type a few letters, and chat with him occasionly. He was forever bustling in and out, doing things that I knew nothing about.

Nevertheless, the surly youth was subdued, if not overwhelmed. He led us to a shiny new automobile, and when we got in, he started the car. We drove on an asphalt lane, bordered by Maple Trees most of the way. It was a very pleasant and refreshing drive.

In my mind, "White Haven" had existed as a sprawling mansion, elaborately rich. "White Haven" turned out to be a cream-white block topped by a pointed grey slate roof, sitting admidst a dainty little garden. The house was made of wooden clapboards, and in its simplicity held a definate beauty. If I had been told that this refined and innocent home was going to house murder, I would have laughed rudely.

"Hello, Mr. Citarro," a woman's voice cood. "We're so glad you could come." A buxom lady crossed the lawn and shook hands warmly with Citarro.

"Charming place you have here, Mrs. Haldeman," returned my employer, with a deep bow after he had said hello.

Mrs. Haldeman showd her teeth. "Yes, isn't it. It's such a lovely location too."

Citarro smiled a very Latin smile and murmered, "But the home can never equal the beauty of its mistress."

Mrs. Haldeman looked at him in an odd way and said evenly, "You don't mean that. You're just acting Spanish." Citarro hesitated for a moment before he shrugged his shoulders and said, "Yes, it is true. My clients expect me to play the dashing conquisidor so I have gotten into the habit of doing it all the time, paying compliments, smiling, bowing."

She said, "Oh, I see you have brought your valet along." I blushed.

"He is not my valet," Citarro said sharply. "He is my secretary."

Mrs. Haldeman smiled again. "I hope that Mr . . ."

"Mays," Citarro prompted.

"I hope that Mr. Mays will not mind sleeping on a cot. I'm very sorry, but our house isn't really as large as it should be, and all the rooms are filled up, so your secretary will have to sleep on a cot in your room."

"I'm very sorry that I shall make you the trouble," Citarro returned. "It is my fault entirely that this should happen. I should have asked first about conditions. I apoligise sincerely. Forgive me." Here he bowed deeply for the second time. "If you wish, I shall be only too happy to send Mays home."

"Oh, no, It is quite all right. Won't you come in."

Although Mrs. Haldeman had been extremely polite and gracious, I felt uncomfortable. It was the second time that day that the favorability of my presence had been doubted.

"Why didn't you let them know I was coming," I hissed at my employer as we walked along behind Mrs. Haldeman. "I feel about as welcome as a toad in between the bedsheets."

"Heavens, Tommy," he retorted, "don't be so disagreeable."

This hurt me, so I said nothing else. Instead I studied our hostess. She was an impressive woman. Her hair was practically white, with a few strips of black running through. She carried herself well, her carraige was that of a being who feels she is always right. At one time she had been beautiful, even now she was handsome. Her jaw was just a bit too square, too pronounced and her eyes were too grey and determined, they gave away the fact that here was a woman who got what she wanted. If I had been 40 years older, I would have thought of her as a member of the "old school."

The house inside was as simple in design as the outside. A wide hallway ran strait through the center of the house, with a door at each end. The stair way started about 20 feet from the front door, in the middle of the hall so that there were two smaller, but still ample halls on either side. "Certainly very neat and balenced" for such a fabulas tycoon as Walt Haldeman.

Mrs. Haldeman directed us into the first door to our right. The room was a large living, or drawing room. It was cleverly furnished in a way so that it would be comfortable yet looked slightly musty and antique, combining the new world of luxury and the old one of dignity and moderation. Reposed on the various pieces of furniture were three people, obviously engaged in the pastime of polite drawing-room conversation. Mrs. Haldeman introduced us. "This is Mr. Manuel Citarro, and his secretary, Mr. Mays. Mr. Citarro and Mr. Mays, this is my husband, Walter Haldeman." Automatically I classified them in my mind. Haldeman was "Rich Men Grown Old", solid, contented, dominated by his wife. "My sister, Grace. . ." I put her under "Sweet Old Paracites" probably never worked in her life, living off of her sister's character. "Mr. James Crayne. . ." "Sporting Old Chap" thin, intelligent looking, jolly good fellow. "And Mr. Merriwether Stone." And here I was stopped. A small, slight man, very delicate looking, with preposterously large brown eyes. They could not be called bovine, for they did not have that glazed look. They were clever, smart eyes. He made me feel uneasy, so I hastily crammed him into Micellenaous and let it go.

It was an hour before dinner, and one of the party had not yet arrived, so Citarro and I joined the group in the drawing-room. "Dash it all, I wonder where Connie can have gotten to. She said she would come up by car after she did some things in New York. I could use the old rattletrap Packard, because she must have the new car for whatever it was she wanted to do. Probably meet some boy friend," Mr. Crayne was expounding to Walter Haldeman.

"Now, Jim, you mustn't be too hard on the kid, she's young and all that," Haldeman easily retorted.

It really wasn't necessary to reprimand Mr. Crayne, because all the time he was berating the absent Connie, there was a secretly amused light in his eyes. Nevertheless, he found it necessary to go on, even though he fooled no one. "This young generation," he snorted. "If only the girl's mother was here." Then a vague sorrow crept into his tone. "Connie was just a little tyke when Maggie died, she never knew her mother. Margaret was a lady, too. You didn't catch her going 70 miles an hour in a brand new automobile, or staying up until the next morning at some wild party. Sensation-crazy, that's what the young ones are."

"But hasn't the human race always been sensation crazy?" Merriwether Stone asked quietly. "Always asking for noveltys, for ways to risk their lives, for adventure. Everyone must work off his wild streak somehow. An office clerk might take dope, a married couple might work off their spirits by having fierce quarrels. The young generation, as you call it, may do seemingly alarming things in the eye's of their parents, but didn't those same parents alarm their parents years back. And when your children have children, those children will think their parents quite old fuddie-duddies. Come, Mr. Crayne, surely you can remember when you did things over your parents protesting bodies, but which now is a commonplace event in modern life. That is progress."

"Well, I remember my first automobile ride. I didn't live with my parents, but, when I wrote them about it, they were so shocked they disinherited me for three months."

"Certainly," Merriwether Stone said, "Who knows but when your Connie is your age, 70 miles an hour will be the accepted rate of speed. That is that alarming phemominea known as progress."

My employer, Manuel Citarro, coughed a little cough, and looked about him carelessly. I knew that whenever he did that, he was about to talk about his favorite subject, himself. "You were speaking a moment ago about people being sensation crazy," he

In the late '60s, youth ☞ confronts a whole new range of temptations. "It's not just cigarettes and a little feeling up. At fourteen now, they're ready to go," says Peggy Fosnacht, the mother of a teenager, in Rabbit Redux (1971).

Rabbit's father is less philosophical about modern-day developments. Had he to face contemporary pressures as a younger man, he says in Rabbit Redux, *"I'd no doubt just have put a shotgun to my head and let the world roll on without me."* ☞

began. "I have noticed that tendency particualy strong in the American people."

"America is the most progressive of all nations," softly spoke Merriwether Stone.

"Yes, that is true also." Citarro spoke a little quickly, as if afraid the conversational lead would be wrested away from him. "I am a Spanierd, born in Spain. But I was taken away from my native country when I was three years old, in 1909. My father was a newspaper man who said some indiscreet things about the administration, under Maura. We came to Mexico, but my father was assisinated for saying indiscreet things about the Mexican administration a year later. An indiscreet man, my father. Anyway my mother died shortly after, and I was raised in an orphanage. When twenty-three, I came to America. I got a job in a factory, and probably would be there yet, had not some papers been stolen. I just applied a little common sense, and I relized immediately who had stolen them and how. Through my efforts, the criminal was arrested. I was surprised to find that I was gifted in deduction, so I set up a small detective agency.

"Now, here is the point of my story. I first called myself Mark Citers, Pvt. Investigator. Nobody came. Then a friend of mine told me to use my Spanish name. So I put out a second sign, Manuel Citarro, the Spanish Sleuth. My first customer was a fat lady by the name of Cranbury. I still remember that funny name, Cranbury. She came into my office a little exited and stared hard at me for several minutes. "It is true," she gasped at last, "That your a Spanierd detective." I thought that this was a resentment of the foreign birth. "Yes," I stammered, "it is true I was born in Spain, but I have lived in America for four years now, and I will be an American citizen as soon as I can." She was an extremely ugly old soul,

Antonio Maura (1853–1925), premier of Spain at several points in the early 1900s. The author explains: "I have no idea where I got the name of Governor Maura. My mother, the only writer I knew, was long absorbed in a never-published novel about Juan Ponce de Leon, the discoverer of Florida, and the house was full of books on Spain, especially in the reign of Ferdinand and Isabella. Hence, no doubt, my sleuth's Spanishness."

but her face lighted up with a child-like look of wonder. Her business, it turned out was a stolen purse. I
found it in her bureau drawer, hidden away under
the sweaters. More curious people came, usually old
women. I learned that there were certain things a
Spanierd was expected to do. He must be handsome,
have a mustache, and smoke tiny cigaretts in a long
holder, he must speak with a slight accent, and he
must throw a dagger. He also should be extremely
charming to the ladies, paying florid compliments
and bowing. I set about fulfilling these requirements.
I was handsome already". Here I looked at him, ap-
paled by this bland remark of conceit. But it was the
truth, even now, although greying around the tem-
ples, he was very good-looking in a mascueline way.
"But I did not have a mustache, so I grew one, I had
always smoked a pipe, but I gave it up and smoked
Turkish cigaretts in a long, delicate holder. I polished
up my manners. I never could, however, bring myself to mar my English with Spanish. I even learned
how to throw a dagger, and carried one under my
arm in my sleeve, so I could demonstrate to my thrill-
hungry customers. Watch." And he quickly drew out
a small, intricatly decorated dagger and threw it at
me. I had been trained to do this trick, so when he
began talking about the requiremants of a Spanierd
in America, I had rose from my seat and leaned
against the wall. When he drew out his dagger, I
quickly made a circle with my thumb and forefinger
and laid my hand against the wall. It was in this circle that the dagger struck. It remained quivering in
the wall. I had hardly expected that Citarro would
dare do this cheap, melodramatic trick in a nice old
house like this, for such intelligent people. It was all
right to show off in his own office, for people who
had come mainly to see a dashing Spanish sleuth.
His office walls were marred by many dagger marks,

and my fingers had many small scars from the times he was not quite accurate in his aim.

These people, however, were just as impressed as Mrs. Cranbury.

"Remarkable," Mr. Crayne exclaimed.

"By jove," cried Mr. Haldeman. "Superb shot." I had always thought that by jove was confined to English lords in books.

"Well," was all Mrs. Haldeman said, and I do not think that she was too pleased with the damage the wallpaper had suffered.

Mr. Stone, said nothing, but his eyes became a trifle brighter and bigger.

Citarro was rather sheepish. "I'm afraid," he said, "that I have been showing off, not to mention doing considerable damage. The mountebank in me comes out at the worst times. I was carried away by the wonder of myself. I apoligise." He bowed deeply.

"Oh, it's perfectly all right. It's not very often that we see a real Latin in full action. And as for that," Mrs. Haldeman gestured toward the slight mark the dagger had made, "We might have it encased and charge admission to see it."

Just then a lovely voice broke into the drawing room atmosphere. "What's this about daggers. Somebody done themselves in," the voice said. I looked up and saw a very lovely girl. Chestnut hair, dark brown eyes, an oval face, a slender figure. "Connie," Mr. Crayne exclaimed. "It's about time you got here. I've been here well over an hour. What took so long?"

"I got here as soon as I could, Daddy," she said sweetly.

"Hello, Connie," Mrs. Haldeman greeted. "Don't you mind him," she tossed her head in the direction of Mr. Crayne. "He's an old bear now and all he can do is grumble about the naughty young generation. Besides, he doesn't mean it, anyhow."

"Where do you get, that old bear stuff," snorted Mr. Crayne amiably. "I got more life in me than a good many of these young cubs that can't use a foot for anything but pressing an accelerator."

"You're dead on your feet, Jim," smiled Mr. Haldeman. "And you know it. Now stop acting like a ham actor playing "Lord Elderbootly" in "The Unfaithful Children.""

That was the way it struck me, too. Everybody seemed to be playing a part, and slightly overdoing it. Here was Citarro acting Spanish, and Mr. Crayne acting the indignant but helpless elder. Mrs. Haldeman's sister couldn't be as quiet as she was, nobody could. Walt Haldeman seemed to have something on his mind, and tried to cover it up by being affable. And into this odd situation descended a remarkable young girl, Connie Crayne.

At dinner, everybody was talkative. I sat in between Miss Haldeman and Miss Crayne. I had planned to do a bit of talking with the lovely Miss Crayne, but my employer, Manuel Citarro, sat next to her, and held her interest. I turned to Miss Haldeman. She had a long, thin face, and her long straight nose together with this gave her a slightly equine look. She had charm, I relised, and a certain amount of beauty but not much force. She was about ten years younger than her older sister, and I thought that perhaps that was the reason she lived with her rich brother-in-law instead of being independent and free. By the time she was born, her sister would have been a big girl, so she would receive most of the attention. All through her childhood, her sister must have been helping her, showing her how to dance, getting her boy-friends, all the things a girl should do for herself. It would be only natural, therefore, when grown up she would come and live

Within the social set of Couples, Updike's ☞ characters observe one another's role playing. ". . . Marcia had taken it upon herself to be dry and witty, when in fact, Janet knew, she was earnest and conscientious. . . ." Also, as Frank helps Marcia, his mistress, into her coat—an "innocent pantomime" laden with sexual energy—her eyes are described as rolling "Spanishly."

with her sister and the rich man her sister married. That type hardly ever married, they were afraid to.

It turned out she was writing a novel. That was not unusual. I never knew a woman like her who was not writing a novel. She took a great deal of pride in it, too, and outlined to me the entire plot. It was a shocking affair, about some poor girl, who when she became pregnant couldn't decide who the father was. Evidently she had several seducers on hand. From then I couldn't follow, but it finally ended up with the child in question an old and wretched bat dying in a prison, clad simply in a ragged skirt and a fearful past.

It was just at the end of the meal that Walt Haldeman announced, "How about getting a poker game together in about an hour."

"Walter," Mrs. Haldeman exclaimed in a shocked voice. "Poker for our week-end guests! Poker is not the game to play. If you must gamble, we can have two bridge games."

"But I despise bridge," he returned, in a whiny voice not unlike that of a disappointed adolescent. "Look, why can't you ladies have a bridge game, and let us men play poker. Bridge is a sissy game."

Mrs. Haldeman's smile was stern, though indulgent. "Yes, but there are only three women and five men."

Walt Haldeman blushed slightly and blurted, "Ennybody wanna go over to the other side?"

"Walter, that's intolerably rude," his wife screeched, and was about to say more when Manuel Citarro interrupted.

"If you don't mind, I would be only to happy to play bridge with the ladies. I, for some reason, can never learn the knack of poker, and I dislike the game heartily. But I fancy myself somewhat of a bridge expert, so I would much prefer the game to poker."

Other exotic ladies' men to appear in Updike's fiction include Darryl Van Horne in The Witches of Eastwick (1984) *and the Arhat in* S. (1988).

As a matter of fact, Citarro could play poker excellently.

"Oh, no, Mr. Citarro, we couldn't let you," Mrs. Haldeman said.

"But I insist."

"Yeah, really," sheepishly said Mr. Haldeman. "I was just kidding."

"I insist."

So Mr. Haldeman, Crayne, Stone and myself would meet in the Game room to play poker in an hour.

As we left the table, I saw Haldeman whisper something to Citarro, and Citarro followed him down the hall into his study. Probably the "interest professionly" touch, I thought and wished that I could go along, but Haldeman obviously didn't want company. In fact, he was rather furtive. The three ladies went in the drawing-room, Mr. Crayne went out into the garden. I wandered about in the garden for a while, then came back into the house. The library door was open, I walked in.

Merriwether Stone was sitting at a small table and playing chess with himself on a board inlaid in the table top.

"You can play that game better with two helping," I said.

He looked up quickly, as if startled. "Can you play," he asked.

I replied that I could. He invited me to sit down, and we soon had a game going.

"Must be very interesting work, being secretary to a famous Detective like Mr. Citarro," he remarked after a while.

I looked up. Merriwether Stone did not impress me as the kind of man who was interested by mystery stories and detectives. But he seemed to be sincere enough, and was looking at me somewhat like a little boy looks at a man who knows Roy Rogers.

"Yes," I said with a condescending air, "you get to see a great deal of interesting things."

"Really! Such as?"

I now was a bit flustered by this attention. "Well, I've only been with Mr. Citarro for three months. . ."

"If you are observant, you can notice many things in three months."

"Yes, that is so," I said. Merriwether Stone now was looking at me with very frank interest.

"To tell you the truth, I am a great reader of detective fiction." He said this as if he were making a great confession. "I'm really very interested how a real detective lives. Especially one so well-known as Citarro. I wonder if you could tell me a few things. Hard facts."

I felt good. "Well, I was hired right in the middle of the Horst case. . . ."

"Your move. Quite a sensational business, that case."

"Yes it was. Solving it established my employer for good. That was why he needed a secretary. So many people coming to see him and writing letters and whatnot."

"Tell me about the case. I read the newspapers, but you know the newspapers. I'd like some inside dope."

"I suppose you know, from the newspaper accounts. . ."

"Your move."

"Oh, yeah. I suppose you know, from reading the newspaper about the murder of old Jake Horst. Found with his skull bashed in with a poker. A man who wanted to get into his shop found him."

"Move."

"There was quite a stink about it in the newspapers, because everybody liked old Jake. And they all felt sorry for his wife, Wilma. A very gentle old soul with white hair and a timid look. Read the Bible a lot."

The author notes:
"'Three weeks' back on page 190. On page 197 he has had time to accumulate many scars. No doubt these discrepancies would have been ironed out in revision."

"Check."

"Jake left a good-sized fortune to his wife. She hired Citarro to find the killer. He mushed around a lot, squeezing all the publicity he could out of this case. It finally turned out that she was the murderer. Took dope. Needed money to buy the dope and killed Jake when she was nuts with the stuff."

"Very interesting. Check."

Thus encouraged, I continued, after, of course, moving my king. "I'll never forget the look on her face when they arrested her. She just turned kind of yellow and whispered real loud right in Citarro's face. "Judas! You'll pay for this." Then she screamed and made a lunge for his throat. This little old lady grabbed him and hung on and hung on. Then there was a shot, and she just collapsed on the floor. Citarro was holding a smoking gun."

"She died, didn't she? Your move."

"Yes. Almost institatously. Citarro felt terrible about it. After that he quit carrying a gun. He has no weapon on him at all."

"He has that little knife, doesn't he? Check."

I scoffed. "Oh, that. That's just a joke. That's just to show the old ladies."

"Yes, but he could kill a man with it, couldn't he?"

This insistence annoyed me. "Yes I suppose it is possible. Of course, you can bite a man in the jugular vein and kill him that way too, but you would hardly classify your teeth as a deadly weapon."

He said quietly, "Maybe you wouldn't. Checkmate."

I was startled to find that I had lost the game, so I said, "It's twenty minutes until our poker game. Let's play another game of chess."

"All right."

Updike's teenage interest in dope finds renewed relevance in the late 1980s when Nelson ☞ Angstrom, Rabbit's only son, falls prey to cocaine in Rabbit at Rest *(1990)*

In his essay "The Dogwood Tree," Updike recalls once losing a playground contest by allowing himself to be distracted and tricked. The contest required children to race, pick out their own shoes from a large pile, put them on, and race back. When a voice in the crowd—disembodied and seemingly celestial—told him not to stop to tie his laces, he immediately raced back and was disqualified. "My world reeled at the treachery of that unseen high voice. . . ." ☞ Here Updike seems to be passing along this painful lesson to his narrator.

As we arranged the pieces, he remarked, "Mr. Citarro must have a great deal of charm with customers. His sucess can't all be blamed on the Horst case."

"Yes, that's true. I've noticed that the same people always keep coming back and sometimes they bring friends with them. He certainly has some attraction. At first, only the thrill-seekers came, the silly old hens and the bald fat men, but now quite a few of the better class come."

"Your move."

I moved the pawn in front of my knight's bishop forward two.

"My, my," exclaimed Mr. Stone. "I've heard of it, but I never saw it done before." He slid his bishop across the board in a diagonal line with my exposed king. "Checkmate," he said happily. I looked at the board, and discovered that I had pulled the "Fool's Play," thus enabling the game to be played in three moves. It occurred to me that Mr. Stone liked winning very much.

He looked at me in an odd sort of way and said quietly, "You don't look like a stupid man to me, Mr. Mays. See if you can't be smarter then you were at these two chess games."

It was a remark that could not be answered. It astounded me so, that I probably couldn't have said anything if there was anything to say. I stalked out and slammed the door as loudly as I could without busting something. The little man had seemed so sincere when he said it. There was no malice or desire to hurt in it. He apparently meant it.

I found myself out in the hall, and not having anything better to do, I walked up the hall toward the front door. On my right, I heard the voice of

The author says: "Properly, 'Fool's Mate.' A neighbor in Shillington had taught me chess at the age of eleven, and for a time I was in love ☜ with the game."

☜ *"He is absolutely in love with winning," Rabbit observes about his golf partner, Reverend Eccles, during one of their therapeutic games in* Rabbit, Run.

Walt Haldeman. Being a very unscrupulous man at that moment, I stopped to listen. I heard the rather agitated, too-loud voice of Walt Haldeman. "If I'm murdered," it cried, "my wife will open an envelope I've given her. In it are named my murderer, and I know who it would be, and proof of that statement. If I die a natural death, the envelope will be burned. So you see, Mr. Citarro, I am quite safe, and have no fears. It is useless to think of such a thing." Then the voice of my employer. "Do not be too sure, Mr. Haldeman. Strange things have happened about murder." Then quite suddenly, the door flew open. My employer eyed me with obvious annoyance. "And what," he asked crossly and loudly, "Are you doing out here. Waiting for a bus?"

I looked my blandest. "Me?" I replied creduously. "I was just passing through to the front door. Say, isn't it about time for the card games to commence?"

"Yes, it is." Walt Haldeman came to the door. He looked a little pale, but slightly pleased with himself. "I think the ladies are all in the drawing-room. See if you can round up Stone and Crayne. Meet in the game room." I looked puzzled. "The game room," he explained, "is the furtherest room to the right at the end of the hall. Not much of a game room really. Just a few card tables and stuff. It has french Windows."

I found Merriwether Stone as I had found him before; playing chess with himself. "Is your opponant intelligent enough this time, Mr. Stone," was on the tip of my tongue to say, but I didn't. I told him that he was to go to the game room for our card game. I found Crayne on the porch.

Walt Haldeman was first dealer. He dealt the cards with a smooth, professional manner. It was easy to see that he was enjoying himself immensely.

He took up his cards with the same degree of hapiness that a boy experiances when opening his Christmas presants. He loved the game a great deal, and was so happy about it that he could not keep the required strait face. When his cards were good, his eyes brightened slightly, and his mouth might quiver upwards slightly. When bad, his features contorted themselves subtly into a mask of annoyance. He tried to combat this by looking happy when he had a bad hand, but he was too obvious. A man who acts in poker is usually a poor player.

"When did I learn the rudiments of poker?" the author asks. "I can't remember. My parents and I used to play three-handed pinochle."

It showed up, too. By two hours, Walter Haldeman had dropped close to $200. The greater majority of it had been won by little Merriwether Stone, but the piles of Mr. Crayne and myself were noticable larger.

On the last hand, Merriwether Stone dealt. I got two threes, a nine, a queen and a king. I kept the king queen and the nine. I got two more threes. Lousy. I couldn't open. Mr. Crayne didn't, either. Haldeman did. He put ten dollars in. Merriwether Stone put $15 in.

"See you and raise you five," he said.

"Pass," I said.

"By me," Mr. Crayne muttered.

Haldeman smiled slightly, and put all of his chips, exactly $325 worth, and a check for $680. "See you and raise you a thousand," he said. He looked triumphant.

Merriwether Stone was not perturbed. He put all his chips in, exactly $655 worth and a check for $345. "See you," he said.

Mr. Haldeman grew very pale. He had been bluffing, and his bluff had been called. I felt rather sorry for him, for he obviously couldn't come across. He was beaten. Merriwether Stone knew it, too. For

In Hugging the Shore (1983), *the author compares the terror of creating fiction—indeed of existing at all across the "abyss" of one's own life— with bluffing in a poker game holding "a nothing hand."* ☞

the second time that night I was struck by the fact that he liked winning.

Mr. Haldeman laid down his hand. "Well, you got me," he said at a pitiful attemp at cheerfulness. It consisted of two kings, an eight, a four, and a jack. Mr. Stone laid down his hand. His only counters were a pair of Aces.

I had thought that Merriwether Stone was sitting pretty with a powerful hand. I relized, now, that he was betting on nothing much more than Mr. Haldeman. But he won.

The ladies bridge game had been over for about half an hour. They had all gone up to bed, even Citarro. It was after 11. I poured my self a drink. All through the game we had occasionally been pouring ourselves drinks, until now the one bottle was empty and the other one was only half empty (or half full, for the benefit of the optimosts). "Mr. Stone," began Walt Haldeman shakily. "I would like to see you after the other two are gone." I was never one to disregard hints. Evidently Mr. Crayne wasn't either. We both left.

Manuel Citarro was at his desk, writing something very slowly and carefully. I walked over and peered over his shoulder. He turned quickly around and looked at me. "None of your business," he said.

"Okay, your the boss," I said. "I may be old-fashioned, but in all the detective stories I read the sleuth at least shows the Watson everything he's doing."

"Do you regard yourself as a Watson. I thought you were my secretary."

"I am." I guess I said it bitterly, for Citarro turned around and looked at me.

"Listen Tommy, I brought you along for the fun

of it. I wanted you to come along so you came along. You've been reading too many mystery stories. I know that this is the ideal setting for a murder. Rich man's country home. Friends. He even has a detective here. But there isn't going to be a murder, so don't start imagining yourself as a Doctor Watson and start prying into my affairs. What I'm writing doesn't concern you. Neither does what Walt Haldeman says to me. I don't want to catch you listening in on my conversation again. Understand."

I didn't say anything. I climbed into my bed. The cot was a very large and comfortable cot. I was laying there with my arms under my head when Citarro spoke.

"How much of that conversation did you hear," he asked.

I told him.

"Is that all?"

"Yes."

"Good."

Citarro was still writing when I dropped off to sleep.

Somebody was shaking me. "Wake up, wake up."

"Eh?"

I opened my eyes a little. The sun was streaming in through the closed window.

Somebody shook me again. Hard. I saw a blurred mass bending over me. It soon resolved itself into the likeness of my employer.

"Wha'?"

"WAKE UP, DAMMIT." Something hit me across the cheek.

I woke up. "What the devil is this. Can't I sleep around here?"

Since childhood, Updike confesses in his memoir Self-Consciousness, *he's been a late sleeper, "preferring to let others get the world in order before I descend to it."*

"Tommy," Citarro said. I noticed that he looked a little tired. "It's happened. Just like you said, Watson. Walt Haldeman was stabbed in the back last night. He's dead."

"WHAT? Good God?"

I hastily dressed and rushed downstairs. Everybody was in the game room. Miss Haldeman had fainted and was laying on the couch. The butler was looking very pale. "I—I've sent for the police and the doctor." He stammered to Mrs. Haldeman and walked out. She was bearing up under the strain extremely well. She had loved her husband, apparently, yet she showed enough character to relize that she must not break down.

She brightened a little when she saw Citarro. "Oh, Mr. Citarro. I'm so glad you're here. You must find the murderer. It was of course some prowler. The police will soon be here."

"I sympathize greatly with you, Madame," Citarro replied. "And do not worry. The monster who did this will be found if I have to do it myself." He quickly added. "But the police are very effecient. I know the inspector myself."

Walt Haldemans body was slumped over in a chair, a little to the right and a large knife was stuck in his back, below and to the left of the nape of the neck. He was sitting in the most comfortable chair in the room, facing the French Windows and the garden. The French windows were closed. There were no signs of disorder or violence. A book he apparently had been reading was laid neatly on a small table at his side. There was very little blood.

The butler appeared in the doorway. "The police are here." Three men entered. One was Stephan Michal Claude—I recognized him from the dope case. He was a very thin man. He looked very bored.

His face was long, his cheekbones high, and his mouth had a very tired expression. His eyes however conflicted with the half dead look of the other features. They were blue, and brightly alive. I knew that this man was intelligent and forceful, and he was a good policeman. A small, round pink man and a bearlike man accompnied him.

"Hello, Steve," greeted my employer. He spoke to Stephan Claude.

"What are you doing here, Citarro," Claude asked. He didn't betray any surprise, but he must have felt some.

"I'm a guest," Citarro retorted.

Claude smiled. "Like in the stories. The private dick is always around at a murder."

"I hope you aren't going to stand out here and shoot the bull all day," I put in indignantly.

Citarro laughed. "Poor Mays. He's so consientious. He's afraid we're going to let the wicked murderer get away."

I blushed furiously. "Well, it's all very well to laugh, but a man has been murdered and his wife and friends are in there waiting for the police, and all the police do is stand out in the hall."

Claude looked at me and said, "You have admirable sediments, my boy."

I said "Oh, shuttup."

Citarro clicked his tounge.

"How-do-you-do, Inspector," Mrs. Haldeman said evenly. "We've left the room just as it was when we discovered the body."

"Thank you, Madame," returned Stephan Claude. "I want to tell you how much we appreciate your coolness and presence of mind. I sympathise with you and admire you in your sorrow." A remarkable speech for a cop, I thought.

☜ *"Talk about self-referentiality! I can't seem to get over my excitement at being inside a mystery novel," says the author.*

He turned from Mrs. Haldeman and said to the round pink man, "Check for prints. Palaferro. The usual places. Try the knife. I don't expect to find any, but you might as well try." Palaferro pulled several bottles and a brush out of his pocket, and dusted the doorknob with a fine powder. He went from there to the outer doorknob.

To the bearlike man: "Call up Doc Dennison, Lassert. Bring an ambulance."

"I'll show you the phone, sir," the butler offered. They went through the door.

Then he turned to the small group in front of him. "Now, then. Who found the body?"

Nobody answered.

"Somebody had to."

"Stephen—the butler—awakened me and told me that something was wrong with Mr. Haldeman. I imagine that he found the body," said Mrs. Haldeman at last.

Just then the butler came back.

"Did you discover the body," Inspector Claude asked.

"Why-er-yes."

"What happened?"

"I was coming down this morning and I happened to glance into the library and I saw him in here. I thought that perhaps he had fallen asleep last night and had not gone up to bed. I went in to wake him and I saw. . . ." Here he stopped short, and turned slightly green.

Claude said, "Who shut the French window and the other windows last night?"

"I did. I came in about one and he was lying very still in his chair. But he didn't have a knife in him. I'm sure."

"Did you speak to him?"

"No sir. When he fell asleep in his chair, he didn't want to be disturbed. He said that he had so much trouble falling asleep at night that when he did fall asleep, even if it wasn't in bed we were to let him alone."

"Were the windows open?"

"Oh yes. You see it was a very warm evening and they had had a bridge game in here, so the French windows were wide open."

"But you locked them."

"Yes, indeed, very securely."

He turned around to the rest of the group. "Did anyone else see him after 12?"

No answer.

He turned to the butler. "Then you were the last person to see him alive."

The butler had become more ridgid and butler-like, recovering somewhat from the first shock. "Yes, I would imagine so."

"You could hear him breathing, or perhaps mumbling in his sleep?"

A frown crossed the butler's face. "Well, now that you say it, I don't recall anything like breathing. . . ." He was silent a moment. "But I do know that he moved. His right arm moved. It was lying on his chest like this." He placed his hand just below where his heart was. "And he moved it to the arm of the chair. I think he twitched, too."

"Were you in the room long?"

"Oh, no. Mr. Haldeman was a very light sleeper, and I had to move lightly and quickly or he would wake up. I just looked at him for a second or two, then quickly closed the windows, and left."

"Where did you go after you left the game room. Straight to bed?"

"No. I closed the windows in the library next,

"The first, it seems, of my many fictional insomniacs," 👉 *says the author.*

then the drawing-room. I had already done the three rooms on the other side of the hall."

"What are the three rooms?" Inspector Claude had a dead look in his eyes, as if he didn't care, but was asking just to be polite.

"Why, in the front of the house, is Mr. Haldeman's study, then the dining room and the kitchen is in the back, across from this room—the game room."

"Game room?" he looked around the room.

Mrs. Haldeman broke in quickly and apoligatically. "It isn't much of a game-room," she said.

Claude didn't say anything, but turned to the butler. "Do you close the windows in the kitchen?"

"No. My wife, the cook, does that," the butler said quickly.

"Were there many windows to close?"

"Really, sir, is this so important."

"No."

The butler quickly answered. "Yes there were. It was a very muggy day."

"Okay. That's all I want to know." A very theatrical phrase, I thought.

The butler looked very pale. He turned the corners of his mouth down in an expression of distaste.

"One more question."

Stephen looked inquirenly.

"Did you kill Mr. Haldeman?"

A look of complete, undulterated horror appeared on the dignified face of the butler Stephen. "L-L-Lord, no."

Mr. Claude, evidently unaware of the fact that he had given near heart-failure to an elder manservant, turned to the other people in the room. "What's this about the card game?"

Mrs. Haldeman explained. "Eight of us held a sort of card party. Us four," she made a vague gesture, which included herself, the two women, and

Citarro, "Had a bridge game. They," she waggled at me and Stone and Crayne, "and Mr. Haldeman played poker. He preferred poker," she added.

"Poker game, eh," Claude said. "Who won the most money?"

"I did," said Merriwether Stone.

"How much?"

"Not that it's any of your business, but I won well over eleven hundred dollars."

"That's quite a bit for a small game."

"Mr. Haldeman and I had a thousand dollar-pot in the last hand."

"Then Mr. Haldeman was the heavy loser."

"Oh, yes, by far."

"How much did he lose?"

Before Stone could answer, I burst into the conversation, much to my surprise. "Inspector, why on earth are you asking all these irrelevent questions? It's getting on my nerves."

There was a loud silence. I was ashamed of myself. "What's the matter with you," I thought. Inspector Claude looked at me, half amused, and said, softly, "What an odd thing to say. Will you please shuttup."

I blushed. [. . .]

As a boy, Updike imagined art—drawing and writing both—as a "method of riding a thin pencil line out of Shillington, out of time altogether, into an infinity of unseen and even unborn hearts. He pictured this infinity as radiant," he writes of his younger self, in "The Dogwood Tree." "How innocent!" And yet, he continues, these boyhood images have not been supplanted in adulthood.

John Updike

Gore Vidal in 1943, as pictured in his Exeter graduation yearbook

gore vidal

G ORE VIDAL, WHO WAS born Eugene Luther Vidal in 1925 in West Point, New York, and raised in the environs of Washington, D.C., has described certain years of his youth as "sequestered" and "remote from any reality." In contrast, the Phillips Exeter Academy in New Hampshire, where he composed the two stories that follow, seemed to Vidal "as like the real world as it is possible for a school to be." He told one interviewer in 1979 that it was at Exeter that he began his identity as both a novelist and a politician, going on to say: "and I've never ceased to be, more or less, what I was at fourteen."

Instead of going to college, in 1946 he published his first novel, *Williwaw* ("written when I was nineteen and easily the cleverest young fox ever to know how to disguise his ignorance and make a virtue of his limitations"). His third novel, *The City and the Pillar* (1948), was described by one scholar in 1982 as "certainly the most significant novel on the subject [of homosexuality] written by an American." In addition to his role as an outspoken critic of society, politics, and letters, Vidal is most widely known for his "American chronicle": six novels cited for their entertaining and demystifying treatment of U.S. history, including *Burr* (1973), *1876* (1976), and *Hollywood* (1990).

The infamous *Myra Breckinridge* (1968) and its 1974 sequel *Myron* were once described by the author as his most unique and immortal creations. Rendered in high camp style, the novels are about two personalities warring for control over a single body through a series of psychical, and sometimes physical, sex changes. Passive Myron is transformed into megalomaniacal Myra, whose mission (or curse) leads her to violate "your average hundred-percent all-American stud," with the aim of altering her victim's sexual identity.

Vidal's juvenile piece about a werewolf attacking and transforming his friend, delightful in its own right, is a perhaps significant precursor to *Myra Breckinridge* and *Myron*. ❧

MOSTLY ABOUT
GEOFFREY

(1942, AGE 17)

The manuscript of this story was found in the men's room of the Colby Theatre in Colby, Maryland. As the author has never been discovered, we hereby feel safe in printing the following tale for what it is worth.

It was on Thursday, the 8th of August, that my bosom friend Geoffrey told me he was a were-wolf. I must say that I, though surprised, took it rather well. "Were-wolf, you say?" I remarked casually. I made a desperate attempt to sound intelligent, but somehow failed. So I sat there and waited for him to answer.

Geoffrey was a calm, efficient kind of person with a legalistic turn of mind. There was little of the actor about him; if he said he was a were-wolf he was a were-wolf and that was that.

"Yes," said Geoffrey, carefully choosing his words, "I think, in fact I know, I am one. The other day at the Claytons' I was bitten by a wild-looking dog. As it later turned out, the beast was not a dog but a wolf that had strayed into the back garden. According to ancient lore it seems that he who is bitten by a were-wolf becomes one himself. . . ."

"But," I interrupted, "how do you know this . . . this creature was a were-wolf? It didn't change into anyone, did it?"

"I wish," said Geoffrey petulantly, "you'd let me finish my story. I presume the animal was a were-wolf, because last night when the moon was full I changed into a wolf."

I sat there woodenly for a moment, and looked at him. He was calm; there was a look of oppressive sanity in his eyes, and a feeling of comfortable security in his receding hair line. This was not a mad man,

Myra tries to reclaim control of the body she shares with her alter ego, in Vidal's novel Myron. *Shortly after making her grand entrance, Myra declares: "Now let the enfolding night ring once again . . . with the ululations of the werewolf. . . ."*

and yet it could not be a were-wolf. I giggled in a hideously strangled voice, and said something like "well, what a funny world it is." I am not at my best in a crisis.

Geoffrey went to the window, and gazed pensively at the nearby woods. I probably should have stated before that we were in his home near the town of Colby, Maryland. Colby is a rustic sort of hamlet set admist some legend-filled woods. The townspeople are kindly, old-fashioned, and perhaps a little mad.

Standing before the window Geoffrey seemed substantial enough. Without turning around he said, "I think you had better leave here before night fall. The moon will be full again tonight."

I had an insane desire to tell him that I was going to turn into a chipmunk; fortunately I stifled it. At last I said, "I think I had better stay here with you tonight. After all you'll need someone to keep you from eating things like . . . like babies."

Geoffrey wheeled around, his eyes bulging. "Christ, what I'd give for a plump baby!"

Five minutes later I was heading for the most crowded place in Colby, namely the Colby Theatre. I felt safe here, until I discovered that the movie starred Boris Karloff in one of his more vicious roles. I am afraid I was not in the proper mood to enjoy this picture; in fact, I did not stay long enough to find whether I would like it or not.

Just before night fall I decided to return to Geoffrey's house. I suppose I felt it was my duty to be with him.

He was seated quietly in his study when I arrived. He rose when he saw me. "Sorry I bothered you," he said. His voice possessed just the right shade of contrition. Together we sat down before the newly-lit fire.

"The moon will be full in three hours," he remarked cozily, picking up a book.

"How nice," I said, with studied calm.

We sat there chatting in a desultory fashion for about an hour. Finally I asked him what he planned to do with the rest of his life. "You know you can't go on being both a man and a wolf. People would talk."

He laughed unpleasantly. "What cure would you suggest my taking?" I told him that there was nothing to get nasty about, and added that he did not show the proper spirit. There was an uncomfortable silence.

Geoffrey stood up abruptly, and began to pace the floor. I was becoming intensely nervous. Several times he went to the curtained windows. Each time he halted before them for a moment, and then restlessly moved on. I began to wonder why I had come back. Gloomily I thought of my position should Geoffrey really become a wolf.

Finally he went to the window by his desk; there was determination in his gait. Slowly he pushed back the curtains, and the wind shrieked in. The moon was full in the black sky above the woods.

He gave a cry of delight; and I quickly placed the friendly contours of a large couch between us. Then the incredible happened. Geoffrey began to gasp in the best were-wolf fashion. He seemed to shrink . . . to bunch up. After a moment of what seemed intense pain he turned and faced me. I noticed with horror that he was covered with dark fur.

"How do you feel?" I asked, trying to make conversation.

"Like hell," he replied. I noted that he mumbled a great deal, and had trouble with his diction.

Then a ridiculous thing happened: he stopped changing. I am not acquainted with the various stages of were-wolfdom, but I am quite sure that one

☞ "The doubleness of things," as Vidal puts it in Two Sisters (1970), has long been a vital element in his fiction.

Incapacitated in the hospital after being struck by a car, Myra (Myra Breckinridge) begs for some female hormones when she begins turning back into Myron. "I'm sprouting hair in all directions," she ☞ complains.

does not stop in the middle of the transformation, and remain looking more like a bearded drunk than a wolf. Anyway, that's what happened to Geoffrey.

"I feel an awful fool," he mumbled, and I detected a blush of shame beneath the hirsute growth of his face.

"You look an awful fool," I said, with considerable asperity, for I felt reasonably safe. Anyone as ineffective as Geoffrey looked could not be dangerous. He did look hideous, though, and I felt I should take no liberties with him.

Sadly he huddled himself into a chair; the semi-claws he had for hands beat the air vainly. "It worked last night," he kept repeating.

"Do you think if you tried very hard you could change completely?" I asked curiously.

"Fat chance," he said, but he did grunt a little. It was no use.

"Well, you're not a very effective were-wolf," I said gaily. He looked at me furiously; I had hurt him to the quick. Then to my terror he got out of his chair, and came walking slowly toward me, his semi-tusks slobbering. "So I'm not a very effective were-wolf, am I?" His voice was threatening; he snarled once or twice. Hastily I retreated to the fire-place, and grabbed a poker.

"Come any closer and I'll club you!" I said. He came a great deal closer, and suddenly, when he was about two feet from me, he jumped. There was a brief scuffle in which he bit my arm, and I killed him; the creature turned back into Geoffrey on the floor.

Suddenly I wondered if the police would call me a murderer; it was obvious that they would not believe in my were-wolf story. Panic-stricken I dropped

In Myra Breckinridge, *Myra/Myron is surprised to learn that during her/ his hospital convalescence, she/he had bitten the night nurse's arm "to the bone."* ☞

the poker and ran into the town again, leaving a trail of blood behind me. For safety I fled into the men's room of the Colby Theatre.

I have been sitting here for an hour now writing this story on a roll of toilet paper. I can hear the police cars and ambulances outside in the street. But I don't think they will catch me, for I have a feeling that I am going to turn into a wolf. Geoffrey did bite me. Well, I have come . . ."

Here the roll of toilet paper ends. Just as incidental intelligence the "Colby Daily" in an issue dated the 9th of August told a brief story to the effect that a mad dog has emerged from the men's room of the Colby Theatre. It was not caught.

Vidal uses a similar structural device, also for comic effect, in Myra Breckinridge. *Most of the narrative is presented as Myra's journal, which Myron finds near the novel's end. "What an extraordinary document!" Myron exclaims.*

NEW YEAR'S EVE
(1943, AGE 17)

"Well, only two more hours to go and it's another year!" exclaimed the Colonel jovially. In the garishly lighted Officers' Club the small party at his table agreed with him. The electric light bulbs in the ceiling were unshaded and it hurt to look up. A small band from the nearby town was grinding out monotonous music. "Too much noise," thought the young Lieutenant at the Colonel's table.

There were many other officers in the club besides those in the Colonel's party. With the officers were their wives or if not wives girls from the town. They were all either dancing, or grouped into parties around the wood tables covered with confetti and the litter of dinners already eaten. "Far too many people," thought the Colonel's wife, squeezed between her husband and the young Lieutenant.

The six guests of the Colonel were trying to be gay and yet listen to the Colonel's stories at the same time. One bottle of champagne had been emptied; it stood now among the used dishes and confetti and champagne glasses. The Colonel noticed it.

"More champagne, waiter!" he shouted. His red face under thinning gray hair shone with opulence, with good will. He was very flushed, and his wife thought, "I do hope he doesn't drink too much. He's such a damned bore when he does." She felt the eyes of the young Lieutenant upon her. Somehow she was pleased.

He was looking at her. "I wonder how old she is," he was thinking. "Forty, forty-five? Certainly not over forty-five anyway." He watched her as she talked to the others at the table. She was making elaborate gestures with her hands, and he knew she was conscious of his watching. She was still hand-some. She was somewhat heavy, but tall enough to carry it well. Her hair was only slightly gray and much of it was still black. There was a little sag about her mouth, but when she smiled, as she did too often, it vanished.

"Have some more, my dear," said the Colonel and he filled her glass. His hand shook and some of the champagne splattered onto the table cloth. "He's getting there fast," she thought, and she smiled brightly at him and thanked him.

"You know, I came up through the ranks . . ." The Colonel was still talking loudly. "He's off," she thought, but she was not annoyed; rather she felt detached. She glanced at the Lieutenant. He was not at all bad-looking. She felt that he would be bald and stout in ten years, but then in ten years what would anyone be like? "He's somewhat like a sheep," she thought, "but such a nice sheep."

"If it wasn't for my wife here . . ." The Colonel nodded at her, and the others looked glassily at her. He was telling them of his life and his wife. "His life and his wife." She repeated the words to herself. They were a pattern, a pattern that rhymed. That's all anything was, she thought, a god-damned pattern that rhymed or should rhyme. She wished he would stop talking. She said something and looked pleadingly at him, but he was too drunk to notice or to care.

"I wonder if I'll be like that when I'm fifty," thought the Lieutenant. It was not much of a question, though, for he knew that he could never be like that . . . a middle-aged bore. The Lieutenant knew that he was ineffably charming. Already the wine had taken effect and he was feeling elated and very wonderful. He watched the Colonel's wife. He wondered about her.

"Marriage is the greatest institution there is," said the Colonel. She shuddered when he said this, for she knew that he would say it again and again. It was one of those trite little sayings that he was fond of. "Blissful institution," she thought to herself, and the words in her brain were like ice freezing her. She would never be young again. She would go on living like this celebrating new years. Celebrating them! God! Celebrating what? Celebrating getting old and lonely and useless. Welcoming the sterile emptiness of new years that would be so very much alike. She wondered, almost panic-stricken, where the time had got to.

"Waiter! More champagne!" roared the Colonel.

Vidal's short story "Three Stratagems" (circa 1956) conveys a similar, somewhat grim, sense of amusement at the romantic mismatch between age and youth. On Key West, Michael hopes to take advantage of his own youth to entice the older, wealthier "fools," whom, he imagines, see him as a "beloved angel" able to "exorcise the graceless shadow of the years." ☞

He poured it into her glass until the glass was full. She drank it quickly. The bubbles made tears come to her eyes. She could forget about herself when drunk—that was the beauty of drinking—to forget, just simply to forget. She felt the Lieutenant close beside her. He felt warm with an animal warmth. She pushed closer to him and he did not move away. Her heart beats began to quicken. "I'm a fool, a fool . . ."

"There's no fool like an old fool," said the Colonel. He laughed too loudly; he had been telling a story about somebody who did something-or-other amusing. The Lieutenant wiggled uncomfortably. "She's probably old enough to be my mother," he thought. He was a very wonderful person indeed, and she was old and spent. Her leg pushed against his leg; he did not move. It was a very amusing situation.

"I remember back in 1916, last war, you know . . ." said the Colonel. "That's all we can do," she thought, "remember when. When New Year's Eve was something more than memory." The Lieutenant's wriggling brought her back. He stood up and asked her to dance. They went out onto the dance floor among the crowd. Couples were swaying back and forth beneath multi-colored streamers. The band was noisier than ever. She pressed close to the Lieutenant, and she could feel the buttons of his coat press into her as he breathed.

"You'd never believe that she's forty-seven . . ." said the Colonel to the table at large. He was very proud of her. She caught the words and was furious, but then she relaxed and no longer cared. The Lieutenant waltzed well, and she felt as though she were floating, almost as though she were young. The dance stopped, and they paused breathless and bright-eyed. They smiled at each other. Together they went into the long room where the bar was. Here was a great crowd, mostly of men. They were forced back into a corner. Someone shoved her against him. He looked down at her through a champagne mist. He kissed her full upon the lips.

The music had begun to play again. The tune was "Night and Day," sultry and moving. She was carried away by the music, by the champagne, by . . . She clutched him to her. For a moment she was blind to all else, and then she saw that he was sober now. He did not move, and she felt cold again.

"Only two minutes to go!" roared the Colonel as they came back. The Lieutenant was pale and silent. She seemed gay and vivacious as she took her place at the table. Suddenly the lights went out and some one shouted, "Happy New Year!" The Colonel leaned over the table and kissed her. "Happy New Year, old girl," he whispered. She smiled at him and said, "Happy New Year."

As in "Three Stratagems," Vidal moves the middle-aged would-be lover toward the brink of foolishness and then back to a state of dignity.

Gore Vidal

Tobias Wolff at about age 15

tobias wolff

TOBIAS WOLFF HAS ALREADY provided readers with a striking portrait of his childhood in the 1989 memoir *This Boy's Life*. Born in Birmingham, Alabama, in 1945, but often uprooted across the country, young Wolff responded to his somewhat chaotic upbringing by continually reinventing himself. He adopted the name Jack (after Jack London), spun yarns in long pen-pal letters, and fabricated elements of his prep school applications. In confessional, he once offered someone else's misdeeds rather than his own.

The childhood described in *This Boy's Life* straddles mischief and delinquency. In one chilling recollection, the preteenage Wolff sights passers-by through his loaded Winchester rifle, relishing his power over them, until so overcome with the need to shoot, he kills a squirrel. He is immediately, if briefly, remorseful. In this elegantly written memoir, however, even his more ignoble childhood exploits are transformed by the grace of his telling, and it is clear that Wolff, in these intervening years, has mastered the art and spirit of confession.

Much as Wolff the boy wrestled with right and wrong (and what he could get away with), so do the characters in his much-celebrated fiction, which includes the short-story collections *In the Garden of the North American Martyrs* (1981), *Back in the World* (1985), and *The Night in Question* (1996). He credits his father and mother—as well as his older brother, the writer Geoffrey Wolff—for the example they set as storytellers.

Wolff remembers writing tales as early as age six, and in school he would write stories for friends' assignments, he told one interviewer, adding: "I don't know exactly at what time the idea hardened in me to become a writer, but I certainly never wanted to be anything else."

The poem "Death," written when Wolff was fifteen, could be seen as an effort to create a little order in his often tumultuous youth. The mannered style suggests that he was engaging in a bit of the posturing that he often relied on in his early years. After all, according to the Oscar Wilde quote that introduces Wolff's boyhood memoir: "The first duty in life is to assume a pose. What the second is, no one has yet discovered." ✑

DEATH

(CIRCA 1961, AGE 15)

The Pessimist has cautioned me, has whispered low
In my ear to warn me of that vague, black-hooded
   knight,
Who steals through the darkness, coming for me . . .
Coming to extirpate my life, and to carry me down,
Into his Black Castle.
There to blind me with eternal darkness,
To bind me for time immeasurable in the dank,
   hideous, clay
And twist my soul in an infinite agony of despair . . .
This the Pessimist would have me know of Death.

The Optimist—he has proclaimed in tones loud
   and clear,
That the whole of humanity might hear,
Proclaimed that the successor of life is a fair-haired
   Apollo
Who hovers resplendently over . . . waiting . . .
To sweep me gently away on wings of light gold to
   his abode,
His green mountain of eternal happiness;
There to give my eyes true sight,
To surround me with timeless beauty
And bathe my soul forever in the tranquil waters of
   peace . . .
The Optimist . . .

When he was perhaps 13, the author wrote a short story about two Yukon wolves locked in mortal combat. Though the story is lost, wolves make a later appearance in the adult author's short story "Poaching" (1979). In it a young boy, whose parents have split up, wishes for a pet wolf. When his some-what overbearing father argues that a wolf would be too dangerous, the boy counters: "He would protect me. . . . He would love me."

Not long before 👉 *composing this poem, Wolff, seeking a way to improve his situation, wanted to apply to prep schools. Faced with the prospect of sending out a transcript heavy with C's, he opted for "giving up—being realistic, as people liked to say, meaning the same thing," he writes in* This Boy's Life. *"Being realistic made me feel bitter. It was a new feeling, and one I didn't like, but I saw no way out." (After getting his hands on some blank transcript forms and school letterhead, however, he was able to enhance his applications, filling them with what he saw as the truth of his hidden self. He was accepted at The Hill School, in whose literary magazine this poem first appeared.)*

And the Realist . . . states flatly that Death
Is simply that condition which follows the cessation
    of life . . .
A condition, he declares; not a blindness or light,
Neither suffering nor happiness . . .
And, he further assures me, it neither steals through
    the Shadows
Nor does it soar lightly above,
But inevitably arrives . . . and is just there . . . and is
    nothing.

Such have I been told . . .
By one, death seems a limitless paroxysm; another,
A never-ending dream of love and contentment,
While a third asserts the presence of an incessantly
    closing door
Which, when closed, shuts me up forever . . . in
    painless, unlit
Nothingness . . .
I side with none; each is so involved in his own
    edicts
That he lives the death which he predicts.

Tobias Wolff

A P P E N D I X

SOURCES, PERMISSIONS, AND PHOTO CREDITS

The bibliographic matter that follows is not intended to be comprehensive; it includes only those sources that have particularly informed this work.

I . INTRODUCTION

Austen, Jane, and Charlotte Brontë. *The Juvenilia of Jane Austen and Charlotte Brontë.* Ed. Frances Beer. New York: Penguin, 1986.

Bailey, John. *Introductions to Jane Austen.* London: Oxford University Press, 1931.

Branch, Edgar Marquess. *The Literary Apprenticeship of Mark Twain: With Selections from His Apprentice Writing.* Urbana: University of Illinois Press, 1950.

Braybrooke, Neville, ed. *Seeds in the Wind: Early Signs of Genius.* 1989. Reprint. San Francisco: Mercury House, 1990. Juvenilia from poets and some prose writers, the majority of them British, since the mid-1800s. Includes Virginia Woolf.

Chekhov, Anton. *Letters of Anton Chekhov.* Ed. Avrahm Yarmolinsky. New York: Viking, 1973.

De la Mare, Walter. *Early One Morning in Spring: Chapters on Children and on Childhood as It Is Revealed in Particular in Early Memories and in Early Writings.* London: Faber & Faber, 1935. Part III mixes many samples of juvenilia, primarily those belonging to the titans of British poetry, with de la Mare's own broad-reaching and poetic commentary. Discusses and/or includes juvenilia from Samuel Taylor Coleridge, Abraham Cowley, Lewis Carroll, Edgar Allan Poe ("To Helen"), Alexander Pope ("Ode on Solitude"), Percy Bysshe Shelley, Robert Louis Stevenson, Alfred Tennyson, and others.

Fitzgerald, F. Scott. *The Apprentice Fiction of F. Scott Fitzgerald: 1909–1917.* Ed. John Kuehl. New Brunswick, N.J.: Rutgers University Press, 1965. Includes "A Luckless Santa Claus," "The Trail of the Duke," and thirteen other Fitzgerald stories written from age thirteen to twenty-one.

Flaubert, Gustave. *Early Writings.* Trans. (with introduction) Robert Griffin. Lincoln: University of Nebraska Press, 1991.

Grey, J. David, ed. *Jane Austen's Beginnings: The Juvenilia and* Lady Susan. Ann Arbor: University of Michigan Research Press, 1989. Scholarly essays, including contributions by Donald Stone and A. Walton Litz.

Hemingway, Ernest. *Ernest Hemingway's Apprenticeship: Oak Park, 1916–1917.* Ed. Matthew J. Bruccoli. Washington, D.C.: Microcard Editions, 1971. The author's high school publications, including "Judgment of Manitou."

Kupferberg, Tuli, and Sylvia Topp, comp. *First Glance: Childhood Creations of the Famous.* Maplewood, N.J.: Hammond, 1978. Includes about 100 entries, mostly from previous generations, representing all fields. Among the authors included are Anton Chekhov, W.E.B. Du Bois, Ben Franklin, Anaïs Nin, Sylvia Plath, and Edgar Allan Poe (letter).

Livingston, Myra Cohn. *The Child as Poet: Myth or Reality?* Boston: Horn, 1984.

Marecki, Joan E. "Bowles, Paul (Frederick)." *Contemporary Authors New Revision Series.* Vol. 19. Detroit: Gale Research, 1987.

Pickard, Samuel T. *Hawthorne's First Diary.* 1897. Reprint. New York: Haskell House, 1972.

Plath, Aurelia. Introduction. *Letters Home.* By Sylvia Plath. New York: Harper & Row, 1975.

Randall, Harry, comp. *Minor Masterpieces: An Anthology of Juvenilia by Twelve Giants of English Literature.* Alden, Mich.: Talponia Press, 1983.

Shanks, Lewis Piaget. *Flaubert's Youth, 1821–1845.* 1927. Reprint. New York: Arno Press, 1979.

Stallworthy, Jon, ed. *First Lines: Poems Written in Youth, from Herbert to Heaney.* New York: Carcanet, 1987. Fifty-eight entries, mostly from poets of earlier generations. Includes Edgar Allan Poe ("To Helen") and Alexander Pope ("Ode on Solitude").

II. BY AUTHOR

Following each author's name, readers will find a list of the author's childhood works included in this volume (if they were published previously), the adult works of the author that were used in our preparation, secondary sources also used in the preparation of this volume, as well as photo information. Additional source material was obtained through direct correspondence with the authors.

MARGARET ATWOOD

Margaret Atwood's juvenilia appear by the author's permission. Copyright 1993 by Margaret Atwood.

Atwood, Margaret. *Bodily Harm.* 1981. Reprint. New York: Bantam Books, 1983.

———. *The Edible Woman.* Boston: Little, Brown, 1969.

———. *The Handmaid's Tale.* 1985. Reprint. New York: Fawcett Crest, 1987.

———. "The Man from Mars." *The World of the Short Story: A Twentieth Century Collection.* Ed. Clifton Fadiman. 1986. Reprint. New York: Avenel, 1990.

———. *You Are Happy.* New York: Harper & Row, 1974.

Oates, Joyce Carol. "Margaret Atwood: Poems and Poet." *New York Times Book Review,* 21 May 1978.

Photo as an adult by Andrew MacNaughton. Photos from youth courtesy of Margaret Atwood.

ROY BLOUNT, JR.

"Dear Diary by Joe Crutch." Decatur, Ga., High School *Scribbler* (newspaper), Dec. 1957–Feb. 1959. Also in *The Scribbler:* "Robot Goes Berserk: 87 Perish as Monster Roams Streets," 23 Apr. 1959; "Roy's Noise," 12 Sep. 1958; "Science Fair Is Miserable Flop," 1 Apr. 1958; "Signs of Spring," 15 Apr. 1958. "You Ought to Be in Football." The National Beta Club *Journal* (Spartanburg, S.C.), April 1959: 14–15. Reprinted by the author's permission. Copyright, 1957, 1958, 1959, 1993 by Roy Blount, Jr.

Blount, Roy, Jr. *About Three Bricks Shy of a Load: A Highly Irregular Lowdown on the Year the Pittsburgh Steelers Were Super but Missed the Bowl.* Boston: Little, Brown, 1974.

———. *First Hubby.* New York: Villard, 1990.

———. *Not Exactly What I Had in Mind.* Boston: Atlantic Monthly Press, 1985.

———. "Trash No More." *Crackers: This Whole Many-Angled Thing of Jimmy, More Carters, Ominous Little Animals, Sad-Singing Women, My Daddy and Me.* New York: Knopf, 1980.

———. "Women in the Locker Room!" *What Men Don't Tell Women.* Boston: Little, Brown, 1984.

Brown, Jerry Elijah. *Roy Blount, Jr.* Boston: Twayne, 1990.

Photo as an adult by Slick Lawson, courtesy of Roy Blount, Jr. Photo as a teenager by John Baker (*Scribbler* staff photographer), courtesy of Roy Blount, Jr.

PAUL BOWLES

"Poor Aunt Emma" and the lyrics from "Le Carré" are excerpts from *Without Stopping,* copyright © 1972 by Paul Bowles. First published by The Ecco Press in 1985 (pp. 32, 36). Reprinted by permission. "Bluey: Pages from an Imaginary Diary."

View, no. 3, series 3 (1943): 81–82. "Entity." *transition*, no. 13 (Summer 1928): 219–20. (The previous number of *transition* included Bowles's poem "Spire Song.") "The Lady of Peace" (part of "Aunt Pete"). *Exquisite Corpse*, April 1983: 8. "A White Goat's Shadow." *Argo: An Individual Review*, 1, no. 2 (Dec. 1930): 50–51 (Bowles's first published piece of fiction). Copyright 1928, 1930, 1943, 1972, 1983, 1993 by Paul Bowles. All of Paul Bowles's juvenilia appear by the author's permission.

Bowles, Paul. "A Distant Episode." *Collected Stories 1939–1976*. Santa Rosa: Black Sparrow Press, 1986.

———. "The Hyena." *Collected Stories*.

———. "In the Red Room." *The Best American Short Stories of the Eighties*. Ed. Shannon Ravenel. Boston: Houghton Mifflin, 1990.

———. "Journal, Tangier 1987–1988." *Our Private Lives: Journals, Notebooks, and Diaries*. Ed. Daniel Halpern. New York: Vintage, 1990.

———. *The Sheltering Sky*. 1949. Reprint. New York: Vintage, 1990.

———. *The Spider's House*. 1955. Reprint. Santa Rosa: Black Sparrow Press, 1982.

———. *Without Stopping: An Autobiography*. 1972. Reprint. New York: Ecco Press, 1985.

Photo as an adult by Suomi La Valle, courtesy of The Ecco Press. Juvenile photos of Paul Bowles supplied by the Photography Collection, Harry Ransom Humanities Research Center, The University of Texas at Austin. Reprinted by permission. Toddler photo by W. C. Rowley.

PAT CONROY

"To Randy Randel" was first published in the 1962 Beaufort, S.C., High School yearbook. Copyright 1962, 1993 by Pat Conroy. All of Pat Conroy's juvenilia appear by the author's permission.

Conroy, Pat. "Colonel Dad." *Washingtonian*, April 1991.

———. *The Prince of Tides*. 1986. Reprint. New York: Bantam, 1991.

———. *The Water Is Wide*. 1972. Reprint. New York: Bantam, 1987.

Photos courtesy of the author.

MICHAEL CRICHTON

Michael Crichton's juvenilia appear by the author's permission. Copyright 1993 by Michael Crichton.

Crichton, Michael. *The Andromeda Strain*. New York: Knopf, 1969.

———. "Climbing up a Cinder Cone: A Visit to Sunset Crater Makes a Novel Side Trip in Arizona." *New York Times*, 17 May 1959. (Crichton's first travel piece, published at age sixteen.)

———. *Jurassic Park.* New York: Knopf, 1990.

———. *Rising Sun.* New York: Knopf, 1992.

———. *The Terminal Man.* New York: Knopf, 1972.

———. *Travels.* New York: Knopf, 1988. (Includes the essay "Quitting Medicine.")

Photo as an adult by Bruce McBroom. Harvard photo by Robert Gifford. All photos courtesy of Michael Crichton.

RITA DOVE

Rita Dove's juvenilia appear by the author's permission. Copyright 1993 by Rita Dove.

Dove, Rita. *Through the Ivory Gate.* New York: Pantheon, 1992.

"Dove, Rita (Frances)." *Contemporary Authors: New Revision Series.* Vol. 27. Detroit: Gale Research, 1989.

Photo as an adult by Fred Viebahn, courtesy of Rita Dove. Childhood photos courtesy of Rita Dove.

CLYDE EDGERTON

"An Afternoon in the Gym." *The Southern Drawl* (Southern High School literary magazine, Durham, N.C.), Dec. 1960. "Buzzard Gets Bird's-eye View of Three-Man Adventures: Chick, Clyde, Burton Lose Themselves in True Woodsman Style." *Southern Script* (Southern High School newspaper), 27 May 1960, 2. Copyright 1960, 1993 by Clyde Edgerton. Reprinted by the author's permission.

Edgerton, Clyde. *The Floatplane Notebooks.* 1988. Reprint. New York: Ballantine, 1989.

———. *Killer Diller.* 1991. Reprint. New York: Ballantine, 1992.

———. *Raney.* 1985. Reprint. New York: Ballantine, 1986.

———. *Walking Across Egypt.* 1987. Reprint. New York: Ballantine, 1988.

Photo as an adult by Marion Ettlinger. Photos courtesy of the author.

GAIL GODWIN

Gail Godwin's juvenilia appear by the author's permission. Copyright 1993 by Gail Godwin.

Godwin, Gail. "Becoming a Writer." *The Writer on Her Work.* Ed. Janet Sternburg. New York: Norton, 1980.

———. "A Diarist on Diarists." *Our Private Lives: Journals, Notebooks, and Diaries.* Ed. Daniel Halpern. New York: Vintage, 1990.

———. *Father Melancholy's Daughter.* New York: Morrow, 1991.

———. *The Finishing School.* New York: Viking, 1985.

———. "Journals: 1982–1987." *Our Private Lives.*

———. "Notes for a Story." *Dream Children.* New York: Knopf, 1976.

———. "Some Side Effects of Time Travel." *Dream Children.*

———. *A Southern Family.* New York: Morrow, 1987.

———. "The Uses of Autobiography." *The Writer,* Mar. 1987.

Hill, Jane. *Gail Godwin.* New York: Twayne, 1992.

Photo as an adult by Jerry Bauer, courtesy of Gail Godwin. Photos from youth courtesy of Gail Godwin.

ALLAN GURGANUS

"Dare to Be Different" (drawing). Rocky Mount, N.C., High School *Blackbird,* 1 Nov. 1963. Reprinted by the author's permission. Copyright 1963, 1993 by Allan Gurganus. Allan Gurganus's piece of juvenilia appears by the author's permission. Copyright 1993 by Allan Gurganus.

Gurganus, Allan. "Adult Art." *White People.* New York: Knopf, 1991.

———. "Garden Sermon: Being the History of a History, Notes from a Journal About How to Keep a Long Long Project Alive. Or:—What I Did with My Summer Vacation." From "Two Essays for Aloud." *Iowa Review,* 19, no. 1 (1989).

———. "Minor Heroism." *New Yorker,* 18 Nov. 1974. (Included in *White People.*)

———. *Oldest Living Confederate Widow Tells All.* New York: Knopf, 1989.

———. *Plays Well with Others.* New York: Knopf, 1997.

Prince, Tom. "Mouth of the South." *New York,* 21 Aug. 1989.

Reed, Susan, with David Hutchings. "He's 42, She's 99—Together They Make the South Rise Again." *People,* 18 Sept. 1989.

Photo as an adult copyright by Marion Ettlinger, courtesy of Allan Gurganus. Photo as a teenager by Paul Nagano, courtesy of Allan Gurganus.

CHARLES JOHNSON

"50 Cards 50." *The Evanstonian* (Evanston, Ill., High School newspaper), 3 Feb. 1966. "Man Beneath Rags." *Evanstonian,* 19 Nov. 1965. "Rendezvous." *Evanstonian,* 3 June 1966. The ongoing "Wonder Wildkit" strip also appeared in *The Evanstonian.* "Individuality, not collectivity, is vehicle for attaining equality." *The Daily Egyptian* (Southern Illinois University), 1968. *The Daily Egyptian,* Johnson's college student newspaper, also published his King drawing in 1968. Reprinted by the author's permission. Copyright 1965, 1966, 1968, 1993 by Charles Johnson.

Johnson, Charles. *Being and Race: Black Writing Since 1970.* 1988. Reprint. Bloomington: Indiana University Press, 1990.

———. *Dreamer.* New York: Scribners, 1998.

———. *Middle Passage.* 1990. Reprint. New York: Plume, 1991.

Photo as an adult copyright by Jerry Bauer, courtesy of Charles Johnson. Photo as a teenager by Charles Johnson.

STEPHEN KING

Stephen King's piece of juvenilia appears by the author's permission. Copyright 1993 by Stephen King.

King, Stephen. *Carrie*. New York: Doubleday, 1974.

———. *Danse Macabre*. New York: Everest House, 1981.

———. *It*. New York: Viking, 1986.

———. "Word Processor of the Gods." *Skeleton Crew*. 1985. Reprint. New York: Signet, 1986.

Magistrale, Tony. *Stephen King: The Second Decade*. New York: Twayne, 1992.

Photo as an adult by Tabitha King, courtesy of Stephen King. Childhood photo courtesy of Stephen King.

MAXINE HONG KINGSTON

"In My Opinion." *The Edison Hi-Lite* (student newspaper, Edison Senior High School, Stockton, Calif.), 24 Jan. 1957. Reprinted by the author's permission. Copyright 1957, 1993 by Maxine Hong Kingston. Maxine Hong Kingston's juvenilia appear by her permission. Copyright 1993 by Maxine Hong Kingston.

Kingston, Maxine Hong. *Tripmaster Monkey: His Fake Book*. 1989. Reprint. New York: Vintage, 1990.

———. *The Woman Warrior: Memoirs of a Girlhood Among Ghosts*. 1976. Reprint. New York: Vintage, 1977.

Photo as an adult by Paul Mandelbaum. Photo as a teenager from *The Edison Hi-Lite*, courtesy of Maxine Hong Kingston.

URSULA K. LE GUIN

The author's juvenilia appear by her permission. Copyright 1993 by Ursula K. Le Guin.

Le Guin, Ursula K. *The Dispossessed: An Ambiguous Utopia*. New York: Harper & Row, 1974.

———. *The Language of the Night: Essays on Fantasy and Science Fiction*. Ed. Susan Wood. 1979. Reprint. New York: Berkley Publishing Group, 1985.

Attebery, Brian. "Ursula K. Le Guin." *Dictionary of Literary Biography*. Vol. 8, part I. Detroit: Gale Research, 1991.

Photo as an adult copyright by Marian Kolisch, courtesy of Ursula K. Le Guin. Childhood photo courtesy of Ursula K. Le Guin.

MADELEINE L'ENGLE

Madeleine L'Engle's included juvenilia first appeared in school literary journals and are reprinted by her permission. Copyright 1929, 1932, 1933, 1993 by Madeleine L'Engle.

L'Engle, Madeleine. *A Circle of Quiet*. 1972. Reprint. New York: Harper & Row, 1984.

———. *Dare to Be Creative* (Nov. 16, 1983 lecture at the Library of Congress). Washington, D.C.: Library of Congress, 1984.

———. *A Severed Wasp*. 1982. Reprint. New York: Farrar, Straus, and Giroux, 1987.

———. *A Wrinkle in Time*. 1962. Reprint. New York: Dell, 1973.

Photo as an adult by Steve Vinik, courtesy of Madeleine L'Engle. Childhood photos courtesy of the Wheaton College (Ill.) Special Collections.

JILL McCORKLE

Jill McCorkle's juvenilia appear by the author's permission. Copyright 1993 by Jill McCorkle.

McCorkle, Jill. *Crash Diet*. Chapel Hill, N.C.: Algonquin, 1992.

———. *Tending to Virginia*. Chapel Hill, N.C.: Algonquin, 1987.

Photo as an adult by Michael Mundy. Childhood photos courtesy of Jill McCorkle.

NORMAN MAILER

"The Martian Invasion." *First Glance: Childhood Creations of the Famous*. Ed. Tuli Kupferberg and Sylvia Topp. Maplewood, N.J.: Hammond, 1978. Proofread against this version. Copyright 1978, 1993 by Norman Mailer. Reprinted by permission of the author.

Mailer, Norman. *Advertisements for Myself*. New York: G. P. Putnam's Sons, 1959. (This compilation includes two stories and a novella from Mailer's Harvard days, written when he was age eighteen to twenty: "The Greatest Thing in the World," "Maybe Next Year," and "A Calculus at Heaven.")

———. *Harlot's Ghost*. New York: Random House, 1991.

———. "The Warren Report." Profile of Warren Beatty. *Vanity Fair*, Nov. 1991.

———. *Why Are We in Vietnam?* New York: G. P. Putnam's Sons, 1967.

Kellman, Steven G. "Mailer, Norman." *Contemporary Authors: New Revision Series*. Vol. 28. Detroit: Gale Research, 1990.

Manso, Peter. *Mailer: His Life and Times*. New York: Simon and Schuster, 1985.

Merrill, Robert. *Norman Mailer*. Boston: Twayne, 1978.

Mills, Hilary. *Mailer: A Biography*. New York: Empire Books, 1982.

Thompson, Toby. "Mailer's Alpha and Omega." *Vanity Fair*, Oct. 1991.

Photo as an adult copyright 1991 by Nancy Crampton, courtesy of Random House. Childhood photo courtesy of Barbara Wasserman.

JOYCE CAROL OATES

"A Long Way Home." *Will o' the Wisp* (literary magazine of Williamsville Junior-Senior High School, Williamsville, N.Y.), 1956. Copyright 1956, 1993 by Joyce Carol Oates. Appears by permission of the author. Courtesy of Syracuse University Library, Special Collections.

Oates, Joyce Carol. "Facts, Visions, Mysteries: My Father, Frederic Oates." *Family Portraits: Remembrances by Twenty Distinguished Writers.* Ed. Carolyn Anthony. New York: Doubleday, 1989.

———. "Family." *Heat and Other Stories.* New York: Dutton, 1991.

———. "House Hunting." *Heat.*

———. "How I Contemplated the World from the Detroit House of Correction and Began My Life over Again." *The Wheel of Love and Other Stories.* New York: Vanguard Press, 1970.

———. *Marya: A Life.* New York: Dutton, 1986.

———. *The Rise of Life on Earth.* New York: New Directions, 1991.

———. "The Seasons." *Raven's Wing.* New York: Dutton, 1986.

———. "Where Are You Going, Where Have You Been?" *The Wheel of Love.*

Milazzo, Lee, ed. *Conversations with Joyce Carol Oates.* Jackson: University Press of Mississippi, 1989. (A collection of interviews and profiles.)

Photo as an adult by Mary Cross, courtesy of Dutton. Photo at age twenty courtesy of Joyce Carol Oates.

WILLIAM STYRON

"Get All You Can: A Parody in Verse." *Scripts 'N Pranks* (school literary magazine, Davidson College, N.C.), May 1943: 6–7. Copyright 1943, 1993 by William Styron. Reprinted by permission of the author.

Styron, William. *Darkness Visible: A Memoir of Madness.* New York: Random House, 1990.

———. Interview. With John Baker. *Conversations with Writers II.* Vol. 3. Ed. Matthew J. Bruccoli. Detroit: Gale Research, 1978.

———. *In the Clap Shack.* New York: Random House, 1973.

———. *The Long March.* New York: Random House, 1952.

———. "Love Day." *Esquire,* Aug. 1985.

———. "Marriott, the Marine." *Esquire,* Sept. 1971.

———. *Set This House on Fire*. New York: Random House, 1960.

———. *Sophie's Choice*. New York: Random House, 1979.

———. *This Quiet Dust and Other Writings*. New York: Random House, 1982.

Coale, Samuel. *William Styron Revisited*. Boston: Twayne, 1991.

West, James L. W., III, ed. *Conversations with William Styron*. Jackson: University Press of Mississippi, 1985. (Interviews and a profile.)

Photo as an adult copyright by Stathis Orphanos, courtesy of Random House. Photo as a teenager courtesy of William Styron.

A M Y   T A N

"What the Library Means to Me." The Santa Rosa *Press Democrat*, 1961. Copyright 1961 by the Santa Rosa *Press Democrat*. Reprinted by permission of the author.

———. *The Joy Luck Club*. New York: G. P. Putnam's Sons, 1989.

Photo as an adult by Robert Foothorap Company 1991, courtesy of Amy Tan. Childhood photo courtesy of Amy Tan.

J O H N   U P D I K E

John Updike's piece of juvenilia is published here by his permission. Copyright 1993 by John Updike.

Updike, John. *Couples*. New York: Knopf, 1968.

———. "Deaths of Distant Friends." *The Best American Short Stories of the Eighties*. Ed. Shannon Ravenel. Boston: Houghton Mifflin, 1990.

———. "The Dogwood Tree: A Boyhood." *Assorted Prose*. New York: Knopf, 1979. (An earlier version of this boyhood account appears as a chapter in *Five Boyhoods*. Ed. Martin Levin. New York: Doubleday, 1962.)

———. *Hugging the Shore: Essays and Criticism*. New York: Knopf, 1983.

———. Interview. With Charles Thomas Samuels. *Writers at Work: The Paris Review Interviews*. Fourth Series. Ed. George Plimpton. New York: Viking, 1976.

———. Introduction. *The Best American Short Stories 1984*. Ed. John Updike with Shannon Ravenel. Boston: Houghton Mifflin, 1984.

———. *Rabbit at Rest*. New York: Knopf, 1990.

———. *Rabbit Redux*. New York: Knopf, 1971.

———. *Rabbit, Run*. 1960. Reprint. New York: Fawcett Crest, 1990.

———. *Self-Consciousness: Memoirs*. New York: Knopf, 1989.

———. *The Witches of Eastwick*. New York: Knopf, 1984.

Detweiler, Robert. *John Updike*. Boston: Twayne, 1984.

Photo as an adult by Martha Updike, courtesy of John Updike. Childhood photo courtesy of John Updike.

GORE VIDAL

"Mostly About Geoffrey." *Phillips Exeter Review*, 10, no. 1 (1942): 7–9. "New Year's Eve." *Phillips Exeter Review*, 10, no. 2 (1943): 3–4. The stories are reprinted by permission of the author and the trustees of Phillips Exeter Academy. Copyright 1943, 1993 by Gore Vidal.

Vidal, Gore. Interviews. *Views from a Window: Conversations with Gore Vidal*. Ed. Robert J. Stanton and Gore Vidal. Secaucus, N.J.: Lyle Stuart, 1980.

———. *Myra Breckinridge* and *Myron*. 1968. 1974. Reprint. New York: Vintage, 1987.

———. "Norman Mailer: The Angels Are White." *Norman Mailer: The Man and His Work*. Ed. Robert F. Lucid. Boston: Little, Brown, 1971. (Includes Vidal's comment, quoted in the introduction to his chapter in this volume, about having been the "cleverest young fox. [. .]")

———. "Three Stratagems." *A Thirsty Evil: Seven Short Stories*. 1956. Reprint. New York: Signet, 1958.

———. *Two Sisters: A Memoir in the Form of a Novel*. Boston: Little, Brown, 1970.

Kiernan, Robert F. *Gore Vidal*. New York: Frederick Ungar, 1982.

Photo as an adult copyright by Jane Bown, courtesy of Random House. Gore Vidal's 1943 yearbook photo courtesy of Phillips Exeter Academy.

TOBIAS WOLFF

"Death." *The Record* (magazine of The Hill School, Pa.), Spring 1962. Copyright 1962, 1993 by Tobias Wolff. Reprinted by the author's permission.

Wolff, Tobias. Interview. "Wolff, Tobias (Jonathan Ansell)." With Jean W. Ross. *Contemporary Authors*. Vol. 117. Detroit: Gale Research, 1986.

———. "Poaching." *In the Garden of the North American Martyrs*. New York: Ecco Press, 1981.

———. *This Boy's Life: A Memoir*. New York: Atlantic Monthly Press, 1989.

Photo as an adult by Jerry Bauer, courtesy of Atlantic Monthly Press. Photo as a teenager courtesy of Tobias Wolff.

PAUL MANDELBAUM'S journalism and short stories have appeared in numerous publications—including the *New York Times Magazine, Commonweal, Poets & Writers, Prairie Schooner,* and *DoubleTake*—and received a 1999–2000 James Michener / Copernicus Society of America Award from the Iowa Writers' Workshop.

A former Managing Editor for *Story* magazine, he teaches fiction writing in the UCLA Extension Writers' Program and literature at Emerson College in Los Angeles.